D0426724

IN DEFENSE
of AMERICA

IN DEFENSE
of AMERICA

Bronwen Maddox

LITTLE, BROWN AND COMPANY

New York   Boston   London

Little, Brown and Company
Hachette Book Group USA
237 Park Avenue, New York, NY 10017
Visit our Web site at www.HachetteBookGroupUSA.com

First Edition: July 2008

Little, Brown and Company is a division of
Hachette Book Group USA, Inc.
The Little, Brown name and logo are trademarks of
Hachette Book Group USA, Inc.

Library of Congress Cataloging-in-Publication Data
Maddox, Bronwen.
    In defense of America / Bronwen Maddox. — 1st ed.
        p. cm.
    Includes bibliographical references.
    ISBN 978-0-316-03223-0
    1. Anti-Americanism.   2. United States — Foreign relations —
1989-   3. United States — Politics and government — 1989-
4. United States — Economic conditions — 2001-   5. World
politics — 1989-   6. War on Terrorism, 2001-   I. Title.
    E895.M33 2008
    973.931 — dc22   2008016755

10   9   8   7   6   5   4   3   2   1

RRD-IN

Printed in the United States of America

For Laura

CONTENTS

CONTENTS

Chapter 8

THE INDEFENSIBLE: GUANTÁNAMO
AND TORTURE   150

Chapter 9

BE CAREFUL WHAT YOU WISH FOR   173

Chapter 10

HOW AMERICA COULD HELP ITSELF   192

CONCLUSION: THE CASE FOR OPTIMISM   210

ACKNOWLEDGMENTS   219

NOTES   224

IN DEFENSE
of AMERICA

Chapter 1

WHY AMERICA NEEDS
A DEFENSE

On September 11, 2001, the United States had the world's sympathy. Within a few years, it had lost it. Iraq is the main reason, along with the conduct of what President Bush calls the "War on Terror." European countries which should be the United States' natural allies now distance themselves. In the Arab world, the United States is simply loathed, with a new confidence that the biggest military power in the world may not be invincible. True, with the violence in Iraq abating, even if temporarily, and with life beyond the Bush administration in sight, some of the overt hostility has faded. But the resentment and opposition to U.S. policies and American culture which had been growing before 9/11 risks becoming the settled political view of a new generation.

The central charge is that the United States has abused its position as the world's only superpower. Critics argue, too, that America has been arrogant and naive in trying to impose its values on countries which do not share them, and has been contemptuous of international laws and treaties carefully laid in place after the Second World War. Many accuse the United States of flooding other countries with its culture and consumer goods, and recoil from the values they believe American society represents: too harsh, too individualistic, and too materialistic.

This book is the case for the defense. My objection to the criticism, pervasive in Europe and, inevitably, at a higher magnitude altogether in the Islamic world, springs most of all from a sense of unfairness. The accusations take the best of the United States for granted while exaggerating the worst, and ignore the complexity forced on America by its size and its constitution. They accuse its presidents of imperial intent, overlooking the constraints put on its leaders by Congress, the courts, and the states. They fear that a monolithic "American culture" is taking over the world when there is no such thing, even within the United States. They blithely dismiss the implications of a world they say they would prefer, with America in retreat.

Even so, why bother to contest the point, other

than over the dinner tables of political London, Paris, and Washington? Because more is at stake than point-scoring. For the United States, these anti-American attitudes represent a real cost, even if its leaders do not always act as if they recognize it. For Europe, too, these sentiments are a handicap and a distraction, leading those countries to fight off the influence of a supposed imperial power when the harder task is to persuade it to stay engaged.

Much of the criticism of the United States is well-founded; much of it is not new. American history is hardly short of examples of high-handedness and misjudgment — nor of the antagonism this stirs in the less powerful. But it is clear that the implosion of Soviet socialism and then the attacks of September 11 changed the United States' view of its place in the world, in ways which have increased those historical tendencies. They have provoked a new resentment among those who feel oppressed by the remaining superpower, and those who feel released from depending on its protection against the Soviet giant and so now feel freer to criticize it.

It would be easy to say, as many do, that recent friction with other countries was a handcrafted product of the Bush administration. That is too simple. President Bush has presided over an administration of breathtaking arrogance and misjudgment, and yet much of the tension predated him—and will outlast him. Europe is setting itself up for enormous disappointment if it expects mildness, even meekness, from Bush's successors. Arguably, that tension would have arisen under an administration of any stripe once the United States emerged as the sole superpower. Antony Blinken, adviser to President Clinton and now to Senator Joe Biden, argues that "a new wave of anti-Americanism was inevitable the minute that the Soviet Union fell."[1] He is surely right.

It might seem odd that a country would need a defense, particularly one made by someone who was born in America but has chosen to live in Britain. But the United States is comically bad at making its own case. It is hardly casual about the promotion of its own interests and its physical defense of the realm. It spends $500 billion a year on its military defense, ten times Britain's defense budget and more than the combined total spent by the next ten countries, ranked by military budget. But to a degree that baffles its potential allies, it repeatedly picks fights, snubs overtures, and offers its critics more ammunition. The Bush administration has fitfully sent out emissaries when some rebuff has suggested that it might need to polish its image, but it has picked these representatives badly. At one point, the president dispatched Karen Hughes, his adviser and confidante from his days as governor of Texas, to repair the damage to the United States' reputation abroad, a miscasting that provoked derision in Arab capitals. In persisting after 9/11 with the appointment of William Farish as ambassador to the UK, someone so shy of speaking in public that he turned down more than a dozen requests to be on the BBC's main radio news program, the administration deprived itself of an advocate at a time when it most needed one.

Other provocations for this book have been professional. I was the Washington bureau chief for *The Times* of London during the second Clinton administration, foreign editor in London from the Kosovo war onward for a couple of years, and now write a daily commentary on foreign news. I am grateful to work for a newspaper which edits out any use of "American" that implies three hundred million people might think the same thing (although for ease of reading here, I have often used "America" to refer to the United States). I have also drawn on my previous work as an investment analyst of media and telecommunications in London and New York, at a time when public attacks on many huge U.S. corporations — critics often accusing them of overbearing behavior — were not matched by those companies' financial strengths or hopes of longevity.

As motivation for this book, there has also been,

on a more personal note, the abrasion of ill-founded comment about the United States, if you live in London, as I do, and are even halfway sympathetic to things American. Usually it is amusing but occasionally sharply irritating; the United States is now efficiently exporting the polarization of its own politics into any discussion of America abroad.

I come from an Anglo-American family, many of us holding both nationalities, and we have spent much time weaving together both worlds: my American mother felt with delight, on arriving in London more than forty years ago, that she had come to the country which she felt was home, while my British father, a scientist, would have loved for the family to have been in the United States for more of the years of the Space Race and the discovery of plate tectonics.

That has left me, in Britain and elsewhere in Europe, sometimes speechless at how strong people's opinions are about the United States when they may have experienced so little of it: the sheer size, compared to any European country, the differences between the states, even the romance and surprise of it. My Welsh grandmother, making her first trip to the States in 1970, said, as we went for a cookout in the woods in Maryland, "I never expected it to be so beautiful."

In the first year of the Iraq war, my struggles to get

my young daughter American as well as British citizenship met with bemusement. "Why would you want to do that to a young child?" said one friend. Another, a distinguished British economist, rejected the offer of a gift of salmon from Seattle's famous waterfront market, telling me that the "ones from Scotland are better." The great wild rivers of the Pacific Northwest produce incomparably better fish than do the disease-ridden, artificially colored pens off the Scottish coast, but my argument got no purchase against the belief that American equaled indigestible. Or, in other contexts, simply gluttonous; British newspapers regularly list every item of the White House Thanksgiving dinner as if it were the daily fare of every American, and portray European obesity as just another unwanted export from the United States.

A Foreign Place

I'm not deaf, I should say, to the sense which many in Europe have of the United States as an alien place—and vice versa—and the reliable pleasure the catalog of differences gives to each side. There is a long tradition of measuring the political width of the Atlantic, generally pronouncing, with gloom, that it is getting wider. In Britain and continental Europe, this practice, which supports an entire branch of political science, draws on a long history of anti-Americanism; on the American side, of delight in its own difference. One of the questions I raise in chapter 3, on American values, is why the United States seems such a foreign place to countries which share its fundamental values.

Globalization has only emphasized the thousand ways in which the United States preserves its separateness: the paper a different size from other countries' standards, so that faxes from abroad are sliced off at the bottom; the 120-volt electric supply shared by only Canada, Latin America, and Libya; the pronunciation of "Moscow" and "Kosovo" unrecognizable to the natives; the dishwashers and fridges proudly so large when the engineering efforts of Japanese and European manufacturers for decades have been to shoehorn appliances into the shrinking kitchens of a crowded world.

It was George W. Bush, when governor of Texas, who spelled out to me most bluntly the foreignness of Europe as seen from the United States. I was interviewing him in May 1998 for *The Times* and had intended a conversation about whether he might run for president; he turned it into one on the alien morals of Europeans. The catalyst was Texas's execution three months earlier of Karla Faye Tucker for a 1983 murder, controversial internationally because she had become a born-again Christian and repented while in prison. "You Europeans don't get it," he said, arguing that the "death penalty works" in deterring killings.[2]

The New Distaste for America

The roots of that sense of difference are as old as the United States. But the new antipathy, even if sometimes mixed with ambivalence (or at least a desire to send children to the United States to be educated), is more solid and sour. In Britain, today's teenagers may have little inclination to join the established political parties—as the parties report, with distress—but many sneaked a day off from school, with their parents' quiet support, to attend a demonstration on November 20, 2003 (a Thursday), in London's Trafalgar Square against President Bush and the Iraq war. Police estimated the crowd at more than one hundred thousand, the biggest in London on a weekday, and the climax was the toppling of a statue of President Bush, echoing the fall of Saddam Hussein.

These days, in Britain, to say that you are going to the United States on vacation, not work, invites bewilderment. Even with the plunge of the dollar, how could a bargain-hunting trip to New York compare with the Croatian coast and Prague, which have taken on the glamour that used to be associated with the United States?

My colleague Matthew Parris, a longtime political observer whose Saturday op-ed column in *The Times* often captures subtle but unmistakable shifts in national mood, put it this way early in January 2007. In a piece headlined "Yes, America's My Friend. Or Is It? Suddenly I'm Not Sure," he said that for his whole life he had defended the belief "that no matter how many American mistakes and wrongs you pile onto the negative side of the scales...there is an abiding national soul — a Platonic essence — that is America: and it is good." But for the first time, he said, he was beginning to doubt it.[3]

The Cost to the United States

For the United States, the entrenchment of these new attitudes represents a real political cost. There are many signs that, whatever the disposition of the next administration, such wariness will persist in countries which have been America's natural allies. In Britain, Tony Blair lost his job, in essence, to the accusation of being America's poodle, and there was no advantage for Gordon Brown, his successor, in seeming too close to the United States, although he did give one strong speech affirming the alliance in April 2008. In continental Europe and Japan, America's solid allies for half a century, politicians must defend themselves against the charge of being too friendly to America.

The Case for the Defense

The case I make for the defense has three parts. First, in chapter 2, on the phenomenon of rising anti-American feeling, and in chapter 3, on American values, I argue that the United States' critics fail to acknowledge the breadth of the values which they hold in common, and which are set out in the founding texts of America. Above all, they ignore the ambition and the success of the American project itself: persuading so many people who are so different from one another to live peaceably together under one government. At a time when Europe's only apparent solution to ethnic conflict is to divide countries into microstates — the perilous choice of Kosovo, the longed for but unlikely fate of Scotland and Belgium — this is a profound contribution to civilization.

Second, in its economy and culture (the target of chapter 4), the critics give too little credit to the benefit to their own well-being from the United States' development of liberal capitalism, capital markets, and competition policy, and the innovation and economic strength America has derived from that. They ignore the differences between their economies and America's, as well as the peculiar costs the Kyoto treaty against global warming would have imposed on America, for example, to the detriment of their own countries' economic growth. They type out their criticism on laptops run by American software, without acknowledging that their lives have been made healthier and longer by the advances of American medicine.

A point I particularly want to make is that for all these achievements, it is easy to overstate American cultural and corporate influence, ignoring the signs of the fragility of these empires, from Coca-Cola to Hollywood, which critics presume are eternal. It is also easy to overlook the constraints America's own federalism imposes on these supposed corporate titans. Indeed, in developing cellular phone coverage and banking across state lines, for example, the United States lagged behind other countries because of the freedom it gave the states to set their own rules.

Third, in foreign policy (chapters 5 and 6), I argue that critics are too easily diverted by the horrendous mistakes of Iraq, the repellent expediency of Guantánamo, and the unconsidered promotion of democracy, and ignore the fact that American foreign policy is still, on the whole, a defense of shared values. They skate over its central role in designing the laws and institutions which have governed the world for half a century. It is too easy now to take the disintegration of the Soviet Union for granted and to resent the preeminence which this has bestowed on the United States without giving it credit for helping bring about that change.

The Indefensible

I have no intention of defending the indefensible: the mistakes the United States has made and the high-handedness with which it has often pursued its aims. Not many in Central America or, now, in the Arab world, with reason, are impelled to take a generous look at the supposed imperatives of its recent foreign adventures. Iraq, as I discuss in chapter 7, was an ugly mistake. America failed to understand the unique conditions of its own democracy and forgot how laborious and painful were its own attempts to write a constitution and organize a federation. There is, of course, no way to make light of misjudgments that have led to the deaths of several hundred thousand Iraqis. The best that can be said is that the intention of removing a dictator was compatible with the values on which the United States is founded, although, as is now painfully clear, its unthinking promotion of democracy can produce unexpected and violent effects which may also conflict with its struggles against terrorism.

No defense at all can be made for Guantánamo Bay, the subject of chapter 8. Both the military trials the administration has constructed to try some of the prisoners and the principle of indefinite detention without trial for those not charged are offenses against American principles of justice and equality.

The question is whether this will be so sustained by successive generations and administrations that it comes to seem the settled view of Americans, and must then be taken as representing the values of the country. But at this point, as I argue, we can still hope Guantánamo represents only the worst kind of expediency after the shock of September 11. Europeans tend to comfort themselves by saying that President Bush's successors will be nothing like him, but this is a self-deception which ignores how much his administration drew on the historic themes of American policy. Yet you would have to take a very bleak view of the United States' commitment to its own principles to say that its actions in Iraq and Guantánamo should erase the record of half a century, as well as the prospect that it will continue to uphold quintessentially American principles in the future.

Be Careful What You Wish For

The second tragedy of Iraq, besides the deaths and turmoil inflicted on that country, is that America has been distracted and deterred from engagement in regional problems where it would have had an enormously valuable effect. That is true of the wider Middle East and Iran, and in the incomplete transformation of Eastern and Central Europe. To recoil from American intervention after Iraq is to throw out the best along with the worst.

Those who dream of a more muted America, one "back in its box," and who feel a sense of satisfaction at the dollar's fall, fail to imagine what the world without a strong United States would be like. The threat to the United States is likely to come not from being overtaken but, as I argue in chapter 9, from the challenge by China, Russia, and to a lesser extent Iran to the system of international laws and treaties which the United States helped create, and which they are skeptical has much to offer them.

Those who fear an imperial America skate too easily over challenges to the United States at home, where it will be absorbed in trying to unite a soaring population under its founding principles. Its population, which has just breached the 300 million mark, is projected to rise to 420 million by 2050, half because of people living longer, half because of immigration, most of that Hispanic. No surprise that immigration became a headline issue of the 2008 presidential election campaign. The prospect of social transformation on that scale would be incomprehensible in many European countries. The change, which will leave the United States with the huge advantage of one of the youngest populations in the developed world, will also surely take it into a more introverted phase, as it wrestles with accommodating so many more people, drawing its attention away from Europe and toward itself. Those who wish for less of America's attention may well get just that.

Inevitably, in Europe, this argument will be taken — from the title onward — as a neoconservative tract, and one in the dying days of the movement at that. That isn't what I have meant. Instead, I intend this as a rebalancing, an analysis of what is indeed different about America as well as an assertion of its liberal values.

The word "liberal" perilously changes meaning across the Atlantic. I use it in its classic English sense of asserting the importance of individual rights and freedoms, and the importance of challenging over-bearing government. Those principles are too easily forgotten in Europe in the face of terrorist threats, and even in the UK, with its long tradition of that philosophy. As David Miliband, Gordon Brown's foreign secretary, has said, the left has become sheepish and subdued in talking about democratic ideals.[4] This is an argument for why the left, as well as the right, can defend America.

For Americans, I intend this book to be three things: It is a portrait of how the United States is seen abroad after Iraq, and of why it is so easily misunderstood. It is an account of the dangers to the United States of the new conception it has of its role since the heady end of the Cold War and the shock of 9/11. It is also, as I suggest in chapter 10, a notion of what Americans might do about it, should they care to try.

Chapter 2

UNLOVED, OR SIMPLY LOATHED

The invasion of Iraq brought to a head a new wave of anti-American feeling around the world. This is true even in Europe, in countries which should be America's allies, and that is mainly what I address here.

Of course, Europe is not alone. But the violent expression of anti-Americanism in the Islamic world is a different phenomenon, even if some of the provocations on which it draws are the same. Arab states' willingness to blame the United States for their own deep disappointment in nationalism and socialism, and for their own devastating failure to develop, has been extensively chronicled, in particular by Bernard Lewis, a renowned authority on the Islamic world, with a pessimistic cast that is hard to counter.[1] So has their revulsion at the cloud of "Americanness" which some in those societies feel is engulfing them. This is not to say that those who see the United States as the Great Satan are entirely a lost cause (and the great fondness for Americans among many Iranians, compared at least to their Arab neighbors, is easily overlooked in the United States), but those opponents are not quickly going to be converted. Nor are those in Latin America, inspired by a long tradition of populism and of deriding their northern neighbor, and who have found in the presidency of George W. Bush invaluable ammunition.

But if any region is going to be the natural ally of the United States, it is Europe, yet anti-American attitudes are rising there. Those feelings of distaste and distrust have a history going back to the birth of America, and they are not entirely irrational; they have often been prompted by real provocation. But in some countries — France most articulately of all — they have become intertwined with a sense of national identity. To act alongside the United States can be seen as national treason and can be political suicide.

In cartoon terms, the European charge is that Americans are fat, trigger-happy Christian fundamentalists, opposed to abortion, wedded to the death penalty, and determined to drive the largest cars on the planet with some of the cheapest gasoline. A lengthy survey by the *New York Times Magazine* caught that antagonistic mood at the end of the 1990s, before the transformation of 9/11, when the United States was envied and resented for its size, expansiveness, and confidence. In Britain, Marina Warner, the author and literary critic, in an essay which summed up the well-spoken revulsion of some British intellectuals for the United States, surmised that "Bigness still defines America, but a bigness grown pillowy and flaccid and fluffy and fat like baby flesh...part of a generalized cult of childishness, fake infantilism."[2]

But more than that (as some French academics have made distinguished careers of showing), some find it profoundly satisfying to portray America as a "non-nation," without proper history or culture, because to attack it is to strengthen their sense of their own.

Josef Joffe, the German cultural critic, in a *New York Times Magazine* essay entitled "America the Inescapable," described how Europe has long seen the United States as a "model to abhor....America stood for capitalism at its cruelest, social and racial injustice...and cultural decadence. And of course for ruthless imperialism masked by self-serving, moralizing cant."[3]

These feelings are deeply ambivalent, of course, mixed with fondness, aspiration, and envy. As President Sarkozy put it, "The French listen to Madonna, just as they used to love listening to Elvis and Sinatra; they go to the movies to see *Miami Vice* and enjoy watching *The Maltese Falcon* or *Schindler's List* for a second or third time. That's the truth. The young people wear American jeans and love American burgers and pizza."⁴ For that matter, more British high school students apply to American universities every year. As I discuss in chapter 4, the United States' worldwide influence was not achieved at gunpoint but because of the desire of people for American culture and exports. All the same, the attitudes are here to stay; to dismiss them as solely a reaction to President Bush and Iraq is to miss both their roots and the reasons why they are strengthening.

The New Mood, Almost Everywhere

The new European disenchantment shows up clearly in two surveys which tracked the entrenchment of anti-American attitudes across the world. The Pew Research Center in June 2007 found that America's image had declined since 2002 in most parts of the world, including "among the publics of many of America's oldest allies." Unsurprisingly, it found that the "United States' image remains abysmal in most Muslim countries in the Middle East and Asia." But it also noted that just 30 percent of Germans had a positive view of the United States, and although Britain managed 51 percent, that figure was "inching lower." In France, 60 percent disliked the United States; so did a majority in Spain. The worst was Turkey, one of America's most important allies, where 83 percent loathed America and only 9 percent were in favor.[5]

"New Europe" — Poland, the Czech Republic, and the other countries released from the former Soviet bloc — was more positive than the old heart of the European Union, but even there, support was slipping.

It is no surprise that Iraq was one of the main reasons, but the United States was also the "nation blamed most often for hurting the world's environment." Dislike of the "American way of doing business" had deepened as well. Britain, Germany, and Canada were particularly angry at the intrusion of American ideas and customs into their own culture, despite a "near universal admiration for U.S. technology and a strong appetite for its cultural exports."[6]

By way of encouragement to the United States, the survey could offer only that attitudes were "overwhelmingly positive" in Kenya; in Africa in general; and of course in Israel, and that "while opinion of the United States has slipped in Latin America over the past five years, majorities in Mexico, Peru, and even

Venezuela still say they have a positive opinion of their large neighbor to the north."[7]

These bleak findings were echoed in a survey of American and European public opinion by the German Marshall Fund, which found that although fewer than a fifth of Europeans approved of President Bush's policies, nearly half thought the 2008 presidential election would make no difference to their feelings, regardless of who won.[8]

The Background Noise of British Life

Why do these feelings run so deep in those European countries that are America's natural allies? Let me start with Britain, because it is the closest European nation to the United States in geography, language, and traditional sympathy. It would be wrong to say that the dominant tone is hostile to America; instead, it is rather a presumption of intimacy, an assumption that anyone knows enough about the United States to offer an expert opinion. But it is startling how often the mixture of affection, admiration, and condescension resolves itself into an expression of overt dislike.

Margaret Drabble, one of Britain's most distinguished novelists, wrote this in May 2003, two months after the Iraq invasion: "My anti-Americanism has become almost uncontrollable. It has possessed me, like a disease. It rises up in my throat like acid reflux, that fashionable American sickness. I now loathe the United States and what it has done to Iraq and the rest of the helpless world." She continued, "I detest Disneyfication, I detest Coca-Cola, I detest burgers, I detest sentimental and violent Hollywood movies that tell lies about history. I detest American imperialism, American infantilism, and American triumphalism about victories it didn't even win."[9]

So what, you might say. But appealing to such attitudes has become useful political currency. In March 2006, Ken Livingstone, then the mayor of London, called Robert Tuttle, the American ambassador to the United Kingdom, a "chiseling little crook" for deciding that U.S. embassy staff would not pay the new "congestion charge," then at £5 a day, for driving into central London. Myself, I think the embassy had a point in arguing that this was a local tax and that — as is the case elsewhere in the world — its diplomats should be exempt, although it presented its case (as too often) astonishingly badly. But the mayor, a maverick with a taste for headlines and more fondness for Venezuela than the United States, judged that the insult would be popular.

Those who object to such attacks, particularly on the

political right, often accuse the BBC of systematic bias toward the left, against the United States and against the possibility of success in Iraq. In my experience, the charge is greatly overstated, but in June 2007, a report commissioned by the BBC Board of Governors said that while coverage was generally impartial, the United States was one area in which the broadcaster showed bias. In the report, Justin Webb, one of the BBC's long-standing reporters in Washington, DC, said that he often had to fight the "casual anti-Americanism" of his colleagues. "In the tone of what we say about America, we have a tendency to scorn and deride," he said. "And I'm not just talking about [President] George Bush, although he's part of the problem. I'm talking about a much wider sense in which we don't give America any kind of moral weight in our broadcasts."[10]

Leaving aside the debate about the BBC, there is no question that there exists a pronounced vein of anti-American attitudes across both the political left and right. It is noisiest on the left, among those who cut their teeth on the anti-Vietnam and antinuclear demonstrations of the 1970s and 1980s, and among those who now see an American hand in the worst effects of globalization. Tony Blair's wing of the Labour Party, which he had painfully dragged toward the political center, is passionately pro-American as an article of faith, although some of its members have become more subdued, inhibited even, about asserting those shared values, while Gordon Brown's wing has been noticeably cooler. Anti-American sentiments also have had a long tradition among conservatives, nervous about the erosion of British culture and identity, although they are balanced by the high Tory grandees, former generals and Foreign Office knights of the realm, meeting in the mirrored breakfast rooms of the Mandarin Oriental hotel in Knightsbridge to affirm their belief in the transatlantic alliance.

The Attitudes Were There Before Iraq

In London, after the Iraq invasion, a bitter joke among resident Americans was whether to call themselves Canadians to avoid getting into discussions about the war. In a BBC online debate on just that question in April 2006, a Canadian contributor said, "If you suspect your 'Canadian' is actually American, ask them to name three provinces (excluding Ontario) or what the capital of Saskatchewan is," adding, "We don't like them either, by the way."[11]

But Iraq only reactivated attitudes that were there already. On November 2, 2001, in a shocking and much-noticed essay called "The Spirit of Terrorism" in *Le*

Monde, the admired French cultural critic and philosopher Jean Baudrillard wrote of his "prodigious jubilation" at the sight of the two planes slamming into the Twin Towers. The superpower had, he said, "through its unbearable power, engendered all that violence brewing around the world," adding that "we have dreamed of this event, because everybody must dream of the destruction of any power hegemonic to that degree."

Meanwhile, in Britain, the BBC issued a rare public apology for the edition of its *Question Time* television panel program two days after September 11, 2001, during which members of the audience attacked the United States for bringing the tragedy on itself through its "anti-Arab" policy in the Middle East. According to many reports, Phil Lader, the former U.S. ambassador to the UK who was on the panel and was shouted down by the audience, was close to tears.

These were not isolated incidents. One leading academic analysis noted "an astonishing indifference on display" after 9/11. "From Mexico to Europe to Asia, the search for rationalizations for the attacks set in, mostly led by public intellectuals and sometimes manifested in barely concealed malicious joy," said academics Michael Werz, transatlantic fellow of the German Marshall Fund, and Barbara Fried, a visiting scholar at the University of California, in 2007. "America, the alleged source of violence and all ills, finally had received its comeuppance for its historical role as a global power."[12]

Why?

Some of this rising hostility, even before Iraq, can be attributed to the demise of the Soviet Union, which left the United States as the world's sole superpower, the "hyperpower," in the phrase coined by Hubert Védrine, French foreign minister, in 1999. Tony Blair, in a two-hour interview with *The Times* in May 2002 which was largely devoted to the transatlantic relationship, said the inspiration for the "anti-American voices" within Europe was "jealousy about America's position, worry about American culture dominating European culture. Also, partly, America is the world superpower. Anyone who is preeminent always takes a bit of flak."[13] As if to rub home Britain's dependence on that eminence, the interview had taken place squashed into an eight-seater plane on the way to Madrid, as Alastair Campbell, Tony Blair's adviser, griped that parliament would not let the prime minister have the equivalent of Air Force One.

The flak which Tony Blair predicted reliably arrived. In Europe, as memory of the Cold War retreated, countries were suddenly able to criticize the United States without depending on it to defend them from the Soviet Union. European countries also became readier to see American action as high-handed. Unfair as it might seem, in the 1999 Kosovo conflict, the United States was accused both of impe-rialism in leading the military action and of refus-ing to get enough involved when it declined to put its troops on the ground.

At the same time, the blossoming anti-globalization movement was appropriated by its most energetic cam-paigners to attack the spread of all things American. The end of the Cold War allowed Europe to explore again its sense that it had very different cultural and intellectual traditions from the New World—that it had, at heart, a very different spirit. Peter Beinart, just before 9/11, put it this way in the *New Republic:* "During the Cold War, Europe resented America for what it did; today, Europe resents America for what it believes, global warming, missile defense, the death penalty, economic policy—each dispute further illus-trated this transatlantic cultural gulf."[14]

Peter Schneider, the German writer and academic, was distressed on Americans' behalf for the sacrifice of soul that had come with their perfection of the body. "One of the great unsolved mysteries of Ameri-can culture is the devotion Americans have for their teeth.... Those with perfect teeth unwittingly suffer a loss. They cannot appreciate the idea that natural diversity or incompleteness is part of a person's character."[15]

Long History of European Anti-Americanism

It is worth saying a word about the deep roots of anti-American feeling across Europe, particularly in France, in arguing why the phenomenon is not about to go away. Britain, France, and Germany were all losers from the "American Century," as Alexander Stephan, a professor of German at Ohio State University who runs a project studying anti-Americanism around the world, points out.[16] They lost empires, territory, and financial power as America rose. But in Britain and Germany, any anti-American feeling was tempered by a strong sense of being closely intertwined with the United States — in Britain's case, with a common language, whose value in constantly affirming that link is impossible to overstate. The old British left might have agonized over the erosion of British culture through American films and music, and George Orwell may have lamented "half-understood import[s] from America,"[17] but in a postwar Britain still dealing with rationed food supplies, America was a land of unattainable plenty.

There were crises in the relationship at the highest level; Britain's failed attempt to get control of the Suez Canal in 1956 did not help, nor did the McCarthyism of the 1950s. But postwar cultural exchanges such as the Fulbright Program had a profound impact on future British politicians and intellectuals, impressing them with the best of the United States. In his 2006 essay "Britain: In Between," Hugh Wilford, an associate professor of history at California State University, quotes Margaret Thatcher describing her first visit to the United States in 1967 as "an excitement" that "never really subsided."[18]

In Germany, dependence on the United States, financially and managerially, as it rebuilt itself after the Second World War mitigated against wholesale rejection of American values. Germany does, in any case, see more of itself in the United States than do many European countries, from its federalism after the war, with so much power devolved to the states, to the structure of its education; from its kindergartens to its universities; not to mention the cuisine of hamburgers, frankfurters, and endless breads and cookies.

Of course, the anti-Vietnam and antinuclear demonstrations of the 1970s and 1980s seized Germans' imaginations, and anti-American sentiment was powerful enough for Gerhard Schröder, as chancellor, to win the 2002 election based on extravagant attacks on the United States ahead of the looming war in Iraq. But the sense of a tie easily restored was always there, as Angela Merkel, his successor, appreciated.

France is different, and conscious of that difference. An ally of America against Britain in the War of Independence, its own revolution of 1789 inspired by ideals of liberty and equality, it has nonetheless, more than any other European country, set itself up as a moral and political challenger to the United States, and as a model of a different kind of nation. France is the Western European country where anti-Americanism is most openly articulated and most closely intertwined with national identity, noted Philippe Roger, a French academic who produced a magisterial analysis of French historical antipathy to the United States shortly before the Iraq invasion.

It is, as Nicolas Sarkozy, now France's president, said with understatement in Washington, DC, in 2006, a "complicated" relationship. France's early alliance with America lasted only until its own revolution of 1789. Walter Mead, of the Council on Foreign Relations, discussing Roger's arguments, notes, "The short-lived period of Franco-American unity during the American Revolution" was inspired partly by France's desire for "revenge on Britain for the humiliations of the Seven Years' War," a conflict which had drawn in all the great powers of Europe.[19]

There have always been figures in French history who championed American values, beginning with the Marquis de Lafayette, who fought with George Washington and returned home to argue for the American way. (The White House, in a heavy-handed and high-calorie compliment, served President Sarkozy a dessert called Lafayette's Legacy on his November 2007 visit.) There have been spasms when shared republican ideals have expressed themselves in romantic gestures, most solidly in the presentation of the Statue of Liberty by France to the United States in 1886. But Alexis de Tocqueville's *Democracy in America,* published in 1835 and 1840, was derided in France for the rest of the century for "sugar-coating" the United States. France backed the South in the Civil War (partly for its perceived Latinate rather than "Anglo-Saxon" culture), hoping to see the war put a limit on American power. In 1898, when America declared war on Spain, France became alarmed that it might be next. That was the point, Roger argues, when French anti-Americanism became serious.

France then resented the late entry (from its point of view) of American troops into the First World War in 1917, and felt the terms of the settlement at the Treaty of Versailles in 1919 left it shackled to American moneylenders (a provocation for anti-Semitic French productions, including the notorious *L'Oncle Shylock,* or *Uncle Shylock,* a play, of sorts, on "Uncle Sam").

It takes some doing to see the United States as a greater threat than Hitler, but Hubert Beuve-Méry, the founder of *Le Monde,* in May 1944, just weeks before American GIs landed on the Normandy beaches, argued that "The Americans represent a real danger for France, different from the one posed by Germany or the one with which the Russians may, in time, threaten us. The Americans may have preserved a cult of Liberty but they do not feel the need to liberate themselves from the servitude which their capitalism has created."[20] In withdrawing from the American-led NATO command structure in 1966, President Charles de Gaulle portrayed the United States as a threat on a par with the Soviet Union.

The New Pro-American Mood Is Shallow

Many have heralded the arrival of Sarkozy as France's president and of Angela Merkel as Germany's new chancellor as the beginning of a new wave of pro-American feeling. Sarkozy, when still interior minister, speaking in the Daughters of the American Revolution hall in Washington, DC, on September 12, 2006, paid the United States all the compliments it could possibly have felt were overdue. "For me," he said, "the virulence of the commentaries in the press and by the

French elites reflects a certain envy, not to say jealousy, of your brilliant success. The United States…is the world's leading economic, monetary, and military power. Your economy is flourishing, your intellectual life is rich, and…the world's best researchers work at your universities, [where]…they quickly turn into American patriots."

Sarkozy added, "I've come to tell you that when a young American soldier dies anywhere else in the world, I can't help but think that he has the same face as one who came to die for us in 1917 or 1944." David Martinon, then spokesman for President Sarkozy, said in October 2007, "Under his presidency it is no longer taboo to be pro-American and to be French."[21] The newspaper *Le Figaro* elaborated on this shift. "What is new is that France no longer positions herself as a rival of the U.S.," it wrote. "She doesn't let herself be locked into a role that should not be hers, as a rallying point for all those who oppose America."[22]

Angela Merkel, who grew up behind the Iron Curtain in what was then East Germany, has been determined to use her chancellorship to strengthen ties with the United States and to cool them with Russia (Gerhard Schröder, her predecessor, promptly took a job with the Russian state-owned energy giant Gazprom on leaving office). But these exuberant claims of a new fondness for the superpower should be taken skeptically. They hold true more of the leaders than the public at large (and despite President Sarkozy's enthusiasm, his own foreign minister, Bernard Kouchner, declared in March 2008 that no matter who succeeds President Bush, "the magic is over").[23]

For all the efforts of pro-American advocates to distinguish between President Bush and the United States itself, there are signs that most Europeans are not so indulgent. Bernard-Henri Lévy, the French intellectual who enjoys his status as the national contrarian for being passionately pro-American, told the *New York Times*, "*Non, non, non*, this French pro-Americanism is nonsense."[24] Lévy argues that whatever President Sarkozy might say, the American project of blending together so many different kinds of people from different ethnic and cultural backgrounds is essentially hostile to the French idea of what it is to be a nation (a point I shall come back to in the next chapter).

Nor are Spain and Italy sounding pro-American these days, despite their intertwined history and large emigrant populations in the United States. When Condoleezza Rice traveled to Spain in June 2007, her counterpart, Miguel Angel Moratinos, lectured her that the United States would see the error of its ways in its hostility to Fidel Castro; in a widely reported response, Rice, rolling her eyes, silently mouthed to American reporters, "Don't hold your breath."

Richard Haass, president of the Council on Foreign Relations, writing about the "recent improvement in transatlantic ties" in December 2007, argued that "This belief is comforting, but it is bound to end in disappointment." Haass added, "U.S.-European relations are not about to become as good or as significant as they were in decades past. Some of the reasons for this are familiar: social differences, including an unequal emphasis on religion and differing views on abortion rights and the death penalty; lingering anti-Americanism resulting from the Iraq war, perceived American neglect of the Palestinian issue, and both Abu Ghraib and Guantánamo." But he pointed, too, to "generational and demographic changes on both sides of the ocean." The generation in Europe that was most pro-American, that had lived through the war, was dying out. As Haass put it, "Fewer Europeans regard Americans as their liberators; fewer Americans view Europeans as their ancestors."[25]

The Real Cost for the United States

These attitudes carry a real cost for the United States. Since the Iraq invasion, the starkest rejection of the American alliance was the decision of new left-wing governments in Spain and Italy to pull their troops out of Iraq, as they had promised, to enthusiastic response, in their election campaigns. José Luis Rodrí- guez Zapatero, Spain's Socialist Party prime minister, took out Spain's 1,300 troops in April 2004, and Romano Prodi, prime minister of a coalition with a strong left- wing faction, pulled out Italy's 3,000 troops in Decem- ber 2006. Anti-American attitudes have also, as I have said, taken some of the warmth off the United States' relationship with Britain, where a politician has little to gain by being as close to America as was Tony Blair.

Meanwhile, Eastern and Central Europe have become distinctly more sour, feeling that their sup- port has been taken for granted ever since they extended a huge wave of enthusiasm toward the United States when the Iron Curtain fell. The Polish government said in January 2008 that it did not regard the United States' hope of siting ten missiles for its new "missile shield" in Poland as a "done deal," and that the decision would be made "entirely on Polish national interests,"[26] although it has since been more encouraging.

It isn't just Europe that is behaving this way. Latin America, in a populist mood, has found new inspira- tion for its traditional America bashing. Venezuela is threatening to withhold oil supplies, while Brazil is blocking the United States' moves in world trade talks and questioning its attempt to curb nuclear proliferation.

This is the puzzle facing the United States: It stands for Western values and Western democracy; its constitution sets out those principles in language of unmatched power and simplicity; it has gone to great lengths to defend them. Yet, at a time when its allies have the luxury of questioning their relationship with America, they wonder whether they share its values at all. That is what I explore in the next chapter.

Chapter 3

AMERICAN VALUES ARE WESTERN VALUES

"Now It Gets Fun!"—that was the headline of the Drudge Report on January 9, 2008, the morning after the New Hampshire primaries, over a picture of the victorious (and startled) Senators Hillary Clinton and John McCain. Drudge was right. The surprise, the adrenaline, the emphatic and unexpected endorsement of the voters—that is the exuberant pleasure of American democracy.

It is not matched anywhere else. India is the only other country attempting something like the American project, of uniting many very different kinds of people within a democracy. Its elections are the world's most dramatic—a population nearly four times that of the United States, crowded in an area just a third the size, rushing to get to the voting booths. But for all the astounding virtues of Indian democracy — not least that it survives, despite constant predictions of its death — it has not been good at delivering the rights and protections of its own irreproachably idealistic constitution to its poorest people and its minorities.

Nor do American elections have the furtive whimsicality of those in Britain, called at the prime minister's discretion when he believes the wind is blowing in his favor (as long as it is within five years of the last polls). Instead, the immovable schedule of the election of the U.S. president, the Congress, the state governors, and the half million other elected officials[1] in America is the rhythmic beat by which the rest of the world sets its political clock.

The American enterprise can appear anachronistic at a time when countries are shedding fractious provinces or breaking into pieces entirely. But it still represents a profoundly civilized goal: to overcome ethnic and religious differences in uniting people willingly into one country.

These democratic principles, together with the individual rights and liberties set out in the Declaration of Independence and the Constitution, are America's proudest possession. They represent the values in which the West says it believes, and which the United States has defended in two world wars. They are worth defending: they are the democratic ideal.

But they are also much rarer than America has recognized, and much more foreign to other countries than the United States has appreciated when it has tried to export those principles around the world. This chapter looks at the difficult journey by which the United States arrived at its own system of government, and why its values and constitution can seem so alien, not just in the Arab world and other noisy centers of resentment of America but in Europe, in countries which say they share its founding principles.

American Values

What is it to be American? Many people would answer that by referring to the values set out on July 4, 1776, in the Declaration of Independence, and eleven years later in the U.S. Constitution. The Declaration of Independence, by which the thirteen colonies severed their ties with the British Crown (and which they approved at the Second Continental Congress in Philadelphia), begins with a singularly graceful statement of purpose: "When in the Course of human events, it becomes necessary for one people to dissolve the political bands which have connected them with another...a decent respect to the opinions of mankind requires that they should declare the causes which

44

impel them to the separation." That requirement — to justify their actions, let alone in language of unforgettable power and simplicity — is not one which many nations have felt obliged to observe.

The Declaration continues, in text of unmatchable resonance, "We hold these truths to be self-evident, that all men are created equal," and that among their "inalienable Rights" are "Life, Liberty and the pursuit of Happiness." Britain, which has no written constitution and whose leaders occasionally explore the impulse to write one only to back away, might be inhibited, if by nothing else, by the recognition that the best words have already been taken.

This is a statement not just of American values but of what are now Western values — an assertion of individual rights and freedoms. But in saying that the purpose of government is to "secure these rights ... deriving their just powers from the consent of the governed," the Americans departed from the British prescription of locating ultimate authority in the monarchy (and, in the English Bill of Rights of 1689, in God). As Jonathan Freedland, the British columnist, pointed out in his eloquent 1998 lament on the failings of British democracy, in the United States, "it is the people who are the authors of their own destiny, they who install governments to act on their behalf," while "power in Britain comes not from the people but on high."[2]

The Declaration's principles are expanded in the U.S. Constitution and the Bill of Rights (the first ten amendments to the Constitution), ratified by the states in 1789. Those texts set out how Americans — or "we the people of the United States" — are prepared to be governed by their leaders: the division of power between the president, Congress, and the courts; the powers reserved to the states; and the rights and freedoms of the individual, and his protections against overbearing government.

It is easy to forget — as did the administration of George W. Bush, it seems, in its approach to Iraq — how difficult the first thirteen American states found it to reach agreement on their own constitution. David McCullough's astute and moving biography of John Adams is, among other narrative feats, a chronicle of the sheer difficulty of that enterprise — of reaching a balance between large and small states, and between the states and their new federal government.[3] One of the most difficult tasks (as Iraq has again unfortunately illustrated) is setting out protections for minorities from the majority, so that democracy does not simply turn into majority rule, or winner-takes-all.

America's own struggles toward unity (Alaska and Hawaii, the last states to arrive, were admitted in 1959, half a century ago) might also have taught it something about the difficulties it would face in Iraq. That unity was most tumultuously challenged in the Civil War of 1861 to 1865, of course. But that war was hardly the final crisis. The civil rights movement of the 1960s tested the principle that if the United States was going to be a single nation, then there were indeed inalienable rights which must hold true within its borders. Those challenges continue today. But for all the difficulties the United States has had in reaching its goal, the vision of the founders represents the essence of civilization: to devise rules to let people live peacefully together and to let minorities live in confidence that their rights will be respected.

Why Does America Seem So Foreign?

The European Union defines itself by those same aims. Its countries have supplied the United States with great pulses of immigration. Yet the enduring theme of its members' relations with America is that of foreignness. Lives have been spent in analyzing transatlantic differences (and sometimes in exacerbating them). Robert Kagan, the neoconservative commentator, in his bestselling book *Of Paradise and Power,* famously argued that "Americans are from Mars and Europeans are from Venus,"[4] and he has a point, although he exaggerates it. You could group the broad themes of mutual incomprehension into four: size; the American melting pot; the relation between the individual and government; and religion.

Sheer Size

The most banal reason for the mutual incomprehension is size. The European Union, even now that it has twenty-seven members and has stretched out to the borders of Russia, Belarus, and Ukraine, is less than half the area of the United States. If you are flying back to Britain from northern India or Pakistan at night, more than two-thirds of the flight passes in complete darkness, punctured only by a dim, occasional glow from the scattered cities of Central Asia and Russia. Then suddenly there is Europe: large pockmarks of bright lights linked by illuminated roads—improbably orderly and shockingly small.

Many people from countries smaller than the United States (that is, most countries) have little sense of this. They have been to the East Coast and perhaps the West Coast as well: if they have children, then Florida; if they are on the academic circuit, then perhaps Chicago. An official from the American embassy in London, talking to a group of British officials, gently used the stock phrase "flyover states" to describe the phenomenon of the unvisited heart of the United States, and the laconic shorthand was greeted with delight by some of his audience, glad to know that their behavior had a recognized label. "That's exactly what we do!" said a colonel. "We fly over them!"

Nor do European visitors always grasp the emptiness of America. The Netherlands, the most densely populated country in the European Union, apart from the tiny island of Malta, has nearly a thousand people per square mile, about the same as Puerto Rico (although the UK is set to overtake the Netherlands in density). The United States overall has only eighty people per square mile.[5] I admit to having felt some claustrophobia in, of all places, the wilderness of Canyonlands National Park, Utah, on seeing that the map handed out by the National Park Service was drawn to exactly the same format as that for every other national park in the United States — marked with visitor centers, campsites, drinking-water points — even the wildest bits of the continent neatly mapped, it seemed. But then, as I looked out over miles of untracked emptiness, it was clear you could die and not be discovered for months; it might all be meticulously mapped, but so is the Moon.

The Melting Pot

But Europe's incomprehension goes beyond mere size: it is the American enterprise itself that is alien—the notion of welding a nation together by ideals, not shared history or culture. It can produce a sense of vertigo in those across the Atlantic to find that the United States has no single dominant city, religion, cuisine, newspaper, television channel, sport, school curriculum, health plan, welfare system, or set of national laws on the apparently fundamental issues of access to abortion and the application of the death penalty. As one academic study put it, "Establishment of a 'nation of nations'...presented a serious challenge to national self-perception of European countries that were largely based on founding myths of ethnic homogeneity and century-old traditions."[6]

You are born British or French; you do not have to justify that by adherence to a set of ideals, swearing allegiance to a flag, or proclaiming patriotism in the way which seems so heavy-handed to European eyes, from the American flags in front of houses to the weighty self-consciousness of those in public office. British politicians, relieved of that burden also because the Queen is the head of state, can seem informal to the point of insubstantiality to American eyes.

Jack Straw, when foreign secretary, dressed in airline pajamas and socks on a flight back from Tehran in 2005, wandered back along the plane to talk to reporters; the man from the *Washington Post* cringed, saying, "I guess it's cute, but you wouldn't get Colin Powell wearing that, or if he did, there would be epaulets on it."[7]

Of course, Europe contributed the great waves of emigration to the United States in the late nineteenth and twentieth centuries. But even though countries can still glimpse their own culture in parts of America, the project of weaving all those strands together remains alien. The scale of the arrivals accepted by the "nation of immigrants" has no parallel in European experience: from Ireland, 1.7 million men, women, and children between 1840 and 1860; from Germany, 1.4 million just from 1880 to 1890; from the UK, at least half a million in each decade from 1860 to 1890; from Italy, 3.7 million between 1890 and 1920; from Russia, 1.1 million between 1910 and 1920.[8]

Britain aside, many European countries are now shrinking and are wrestling with whether to rely on immigrants to do the work that their own aging populations cannot—and to pay for the pensions. With a sense of nationality so heavily based on shared history and culture, these countries can find it very hard to accommodate the new arrivals, particularly if they are from Muslim countries with very different customs and values.

Even now, the United States' future continues to be shaped by immigration, on a scale which European countries would find hard to accommodate. America is the fastest-growing country in the developed world. According to the U.S. Census Bureau's estimate for 2005, 45 percent of American children under the age of five belong to minority groups.

So, generalizations about "Americans," particularly when based on brief experience of one or two states, are the cultural equivalent of the blind man and the elephant: an extrapolation over 300 million people which is nonsense when the principle on which the country is founded is the uniting of diversity.

One Person Against the Government

If there is one criticism above all others which Europeans hurl at the United States, it is that America embraces a harsh individualism. There is no government safety net for the poorest, they argue, and there is, unfortunately, no lack of ugly examples of American poverty to illustrate their claim. Americans, the logic continues, care only for themselves and decline to lend a helping hand except when doing so benefits the donor.

This charge does capture something of the countries' different attitudes toward the responsibility of government for the individual, although in practice, the details can be less than the bald philosophy suggests. To take one example, Giles Whittell, a colleague of mine at *The Times,* in an article criticizing Michael Moore's film *Sicko,* pointed out that the much-lauded National Health Service in Britain costs taxpayers $1,155 a month for a family of two adults and two children, about $400 more than a good private health insurance package in the United States for the same size family.[9] The NHS's pride is that it covers everyone, but for taxpayers, it is not cheap. The criticism also ignores the part America's communities, churches, and charitable giving play in taking on the role that, in Europe's social democracies, is borne by the government.

States' Rights

As a journalist writing about the United States, I find that the hardest things to explain to a British readership are Congress and the states. People often assume that the president can do whatever he wants, and attribute actions to him alone which in fact represent a constraint imposed on him. In presidential elections, the appearance of governors as candidates is a reliable source of astonishment outside America; these unknowns have appeared from nowhere, it seems, and yet pitch for the presidency with all the confidence of someone who has been running the equivalent of a small country for years.

Americans do not tend to realize, for their part, how much they are oriented toward local decisions—on taxes, schools, and employment rules—whereas people in other countries find their sense of direction by looking toward the center. The strength of the United States' federal system is that it tolerates much more difference between the states—say, on application of the death penalty or environmental law—than Europe allows in its own union.

Critics of America would say that a country which cannot agree within itself on those matters does not deserve to call itself a country, but its tolerance of enormous variation within its federation has given it the flexibility to sustain a democracy over three hundred million people and three thousand miles.

Religion

Perhaps the greatest difference of all between one side of the Atlantic and the other is the attitude toward religion. There are, of course, regular surveys that show Europeans do not go to church while Americans do, and marvel at the starkness of the difference. However, the American picture is more complicated than the usual caricature; a recent survey noted both the huge diversity of American religion and its fluidity. More than 40 percent of Americans had left the faith in which they were raised in favor of another religion, a different church, or no religion at all, the Pew Research Center found in February 2008.[10]

The difference in religious commitment on either side of the Atlantic reflects a deeper difference about the relationship between religion and the state. In America, the Constitution protects a person's freedom to practice religion — any religion — from the state. In contrast, the European Union has been heavily influenced by France, implacably opposed since the 1789 revolution to any role for the church in state affairs. The European Union's attitude, enshrined in its 2007 constitutional treaty, is that the state should be protected from the potentially malign influence of religion; deeply Catholic Poland mounted a fierce challenge to that secular principle but lost. George Weigel, a Catholic theologian at the Ethics and Public Policy Center in Washington, DC, discussing his book *The Cube and the Cathedral: Europe, America, and Politics Without God* at the Council on Foreign Relations in Washington, DC, recoiled from what he saw, in the European Union's decision, as a "curious view of history that had a political program behind it, and that was the idea that the only European public space…was a thoroughly secularized space."[11]

These subtle differences in attitude toward religion are a fruitful source of friction and misunderstanding between America and Europe. Abortion will never, in Europe, generate the heat that it has for decades in the United States. And Europe's emphatic rejection of the death penalty did not spring from religious principles of preserving life but from secular notions of the values a civilized state ought to uphold. In foreign policy, as I shall discuss in chapter 5, America's Puritan roots have instilled in some of its leaders a conviction of their special mission to shape the world that jars, to say the least, with the targets of their efforts.

A Better Kind of Democracy

It would be too indulgent of the shortcomings of European democracies to say that they have simply followed a different model. They frequently fail to uphold the rights and freedoms in which they say they believe. Britain, in the casualness with which Tony Blair's government set aside individual rights and protections that have lasted for centuries, could head the line of offenders. Blair could do this because British constitutional law provides few checks and balances on the executive. The phrase "elective dictatorship" has been used to describe the way a British prime minister with a majority in the House of Commons can write legislation and count on it being passed.[12] When Tony Blair decided to take Britain into the Iraq war by the United States' side, he faced a challenge from his own Labour Party in the Commons, but having survived that, he faced no constraints, not needing even the approval of the budget which the U.S. president requires from Congress.

Blair strengthened the power of the prime minister even further in 1999 when he removed the 700-year-old right of "hereditary peers" to sit in the House of Lords and to vote on legislation, replacing them with people nominated mainly by the governing party of the day—that is, those sympathetic to his Labour Party. It is impossible to defend the principle of hereditary members of a legislature, holding their position simply by birth, but they did have a stubborn independence from the government of the day, a quality that is hard to come by. A Saudi diplomat, observing Blair's move, said, "If that is what he means by democracy—getting rid of one house of parliament and replacing it with his friends—we could do that tomorrow."[13] British governments have only recently considered seriously the notion of an elected House of Lords, which would give that chamber more legitimacy and allow it to challenge the Commons. They worry that it would produce gridlock. The example of the United States, which has managed to be the world's most successful economy and its dominant power and yet avoids paralysis, cuts no ice—but it should.

Nor is France, for all the self-conscious idealism of its own republican roots, in a better position to defend the health of its democracy. The president is hugely powerful; the authority of the office was designed to suit General de Gaulle, not French citizens. Although the president is directly elected, the government he chooses is answerable to parliament, which has comparatively little power. The lack of accountability means that, too often, people feel that strikes or riots are the only ways to have a voice.

The point is not that American democracy is perfect—far from it. The political process in the United States is distorted by disenfranchisement, gerrymandering, and lobbying. But in obliging the president to work with Congress and local leaders, the system respects the rights of individuals and reflects their beliefs and desires.

Democracy on the Grand Scale

It is worth defending not just American democratic principles but the ambition of putting them into practice on the grand scale, not in miniature. European countries are not just smaller than the United States; they are getting smaller. Their proposed solution to ethnic or cultural tension is to break up: Kosovo from Serbia; Scotland from the UK; Belgium into its Dutch-speaking and French-speaking parts; Spain shedding the Basque Country; Ukraine into its Russian and European halves.

This prescription is now often suggested wherever there is ethnic tension—in Pakistan, say, or in Iraq. As Fareed Zakaria, the *Newsweek* columnist, put it, "With the end of the battle of ideologies—communism, socialism, liberalism—human beings' oldest identities have moved to the core of politics."[14] Europe's own painful struggles to form a union show the inescapable difficulty of trying to knit together different groups—the impossibility, even, if there is no real urgency behind the project. Lord Kerr, the former top civil servant of Britain's Foreign and Commonwealth Office who took on the job of drafting the European Union's own constitution in 2001, said in 2005 that the project had been too ambitious. "We tried to do it all," he said. "It got out of control." He added that his next job, of writing a constitution to knit together the twin arms of the Anglo-Dutch oil giant Shell, was "the one that's going to work."[15] No wonder that it often seems easier not even to try, and to break up fractious territories into small cells in the hope that homogeneity will bring peace.

We should regret that. It is true that the advantages of being a large country are less than they were, now that open capital markets and free-trading zones are available to smaller nations. But there is no substitute for size when it comes to defense; the United States is entirely justified in its lament that Europe does not shoulder its share of the burden, but it is mounting a futile campaign—small countries are simply not going to fill that gap. And concern about defense is merely a practical objection to the spread of microstates. The greater loss would be to have let slip America's ambitious ideal of democracy writ large.

America is not alone as a giant democracy, of course; India enjoys its status as the world's largest democracy, and its achievement has been a subversive inspiration. One Saudi diplomat told me of the shock in his country at the Indian elections of 1996, when the Hindu nationalist BJP turfed out the old-establishment Congress Party. Indians have a low social status in the Gulf, "but here they were, running an election of hundreds of millions of people, and changing their government without killing everyone. People here started thinking that if they can do it, why can't we?"[16] But India's experience does not make democracy look easy. As Ramachandra Guha put it in his exhilarating history *India After Gandhi,* the country has been tormented by prophesies that each election was its last, and that it was about to shake itself apart into different shards of religion, language, and caste.[17]

You cannot fault India on idealism; its constitution of 1950, the longest of any independent nation, with 395 articles, borrows heavily from the founding texts of the United States, including the Bill of Rights. It sets out a federal structure for government, an independent judiciary, and, inspired by the prescriptions of Mohandas Gandhi, its founding father, includes many clauses on social justice and affirmative action for the poorest. But it has shockingly failed to enforce its principles of equality, and rural areas are in effect another country, imprisoned by caste to a degree an outsider can only glimpse. All the same, the ideal remains inspiring, even if the troubled reality is a reminder of the United States' astounding achievement.

I shall look at the problems in America's promotion

of democracy in chapter 5, on foreign policy. But it would be a deeply unfortunate consequence of Iraq if America became inhibited in advocating its own values and its own system of government. Apart from anything else, they have produced the world's greatest economic success, the subject of the next chapter.

Chapter 4

FOR RICHER,
FOR POORER

"Wounded giant" was the label, overdefinite and full of schadenfreude, slapped on the United States in early 2008 by commentators at Davos, the yearly gathering of world leaders and business chiefs in a small town in the eastern Swiss Alps. Anti-globalization protesters had splattered the back of one auditorium with red paint in their decade-old tradition, but overt hostility against the United States was much more muted than in past years, even if the subject of American dominance itself led the agenda.

The reasons for the change were inescapable to any reader of the world's newspapers, never mind to this gathering of excessive financial literacy. The dollar was sliding against the euro and the yen. China, Russia, and the Gulf Arab countries, buoyed up by five years of oil rising to nearly $100 a barrel, were circling, looking for a home for their cash and American assets to buy, and bailing out Wall Street banks. George Soros, the financier, called it "the worst market crisis in sixty years."[1]

But prophecies of the United States' decline can easily be exaggerated, as portraits of its dominance in recent decades also have been. The arena of economy, corporations, and culture elicits more strongly than any other a troubling mixture of feelings toward America: envy, admiration, desire, resentment, revulsion, and misunderstanding. It touches ordinary people in other countries where American foreign policy may not, and their resentment is often expressed as a sense of powerlessness at keeping the American giant at bay.

Some of that is entirely understandable. The unraveling of the Soviet Union was license for economic triumphalism in the United States—a conviction that it had perfected the system of economic relations between people. "The U.S. is now leading the way with a new economic paradigm," declared the National Economic Council, which advises the president, in June 1997 at the gathering in Denver of the world's most powerful democracies, an exercise in boasting so unashamed that it brought blunt, formal complaints from European, Japanese, and Canadian delegates. America scarcely needed support from the disintegration of its rival, however, given the evidence from its own citizens' standard of living (outstripped only in Liechtenstein and Luxembourg) and the military power its economic strength supported.

Some found this triumphalism unbearably provocative. The anti-globalization movement of the past decade, a curious tangle of antipoverty campaigners, environmentalists, and self-described anarchists as well as union workers and those who would directly suffer from the fall of trade barriers, seized on the United States and its best-known international companies as its prime target. Their arguments were deeply confused about the supposed damage caused by economic growth, but their attack meshed well with the antagonism people in many countries felt about the intrusion of American culture. The "No Logo" movement railed against McDonald's, Coca-Cola, Starbucks, Hollywood, and other footprints left by the American giant.

But these critics, whether out of idealism or self-interest, give only cursory acknowledgment to the contribution America has made to world growth and living standards elsewhere — or dispute it altogether. They skate over the efforts the United States has made to open up trade or argue that these efforts have hurt the world's poorest, denying any benefit to their own countries of American trade policies. They ignore the United States' historic contribution in the development of corporations and capital markets, and in the promotion of competition.

The resentment also caricatures America as a model of pure free-market capitalism. This portrait of the ruthless pursuit of profit does not allow for the United States' high degree of regulation and intervention in its own markets, as the financial turmoil of early 2008 showed. It also exaggerates America's proficiency (something America itself is not beyond doing). It does not allow for the way that the United States, despite its image of being on the leading edge of modernity, has often lagged behind other countries in such modern skills as banking and telecommunications, the price it pays for its own federalism and antitrust rules. Indeed, it was a comedy for decades that in the heart of world capitalism you could not use a checkbook across state borders; that cell phones were far less common (and reliable) than in Japan or Europe; and that the use of broadband lagged (and still lags) well behind other nations.

The United States' share of the world economy, which has held steady at about 27 percent for a decade, is now slowly beginning to fall as others overtake it. But it still remains the world's most astonishing success story of the pursuit of prosperity and well-being.

The record of the twentieth century—the "American Century"—underpins the United States' claim to have demonstrated the unrivaled success of the liberal market economy, based on an individual's right to own property, respect for the rule of law, and allowing private investment and innovation a free hand. It would be a pity not to draw the right lessons from this, although it is remarkable how many resist doing just that.

Giant

The United States overtook Britain as the world's largest economy during the 1880s, the start of three decades of international economic integration and liberalization which were seen, at that point, as all but irreversible until they were halted in the disaster of the First World War. America was Europe's banker in the recovery from that catastrophe and in the reconstruction after the Second World War.

In the past century, the United States set the rules and helped establish the institutions which shaped the West's economic organization. These included the 1944 Bretton Woods Agreements to govern financial relations between the main industrial countries, and the World Bank and the International Monetary

Fund, both of which began operating in 1946. Domestic policy had international impact as well. The Sherman Antitrust Act of 1890, along with the Clayton Antitrust and Federal Trade Commission Acts of 1914, laid the framework of modern American business regulation, restraining the creation of monopolies or other moves that would undermine competition, and they heavily influenced international corporate regulation as it developed.

The World's Most Famous Brands

It is easy to see why so many have found provocation in the ubiquity of American brands. United States companies are among the world's largest and most famous. Coca-Cola, sold in the United States since 1886, is now found in more than two hundred countries,[2] and McDonald's reported 31,000 restaurants worldwide in 2006. Hollywood, after several decades of aggressive expansion outside the United States, now earns 60 percent of its revenues from other countries. And a Fortune 500 survey in 2007 which ranked the world's biggest companies by revenue put Wal-Mart in first place, with revenues of $351 billion, unimpeded, it seems, by a reputation in Europe for controversial employment practices and for selling guns (in the United States) cheaply and easily.[3]

This reach and level of recognition around the world is not always matched by financial success or by future prospects of growth. Wal-Mart's profits, while hardly nothing at $11 billion, were less than a third of ExxonMobil's, in second place. And while General Motors made fifth place and General Electric eleventh, the list was dominated by oil companies, the result of oil at nearly $100 a barrel.

But still, there are enough superlatives to rub home the lecture on American exceptionalism. The one that stings most, for many countries, is the annual tally of Nobel laureates in the sciences. These are prizes — devoid of ideology, representing intellectual achievement and the promise of future technological wealth — that no leader would turn down except those sitting in Waziristan caves plotting the replacement of the West with an Islamic caliphate. Researchers from the United States won all the science prizes in 2006; in most years, American-based scientists will win half or two-thirds. Gunnar Öquist, the permanent secretary for the Royal Swedish Academy of Sciences, which oversees the science Nobel Prizes, said after the American clean sweep of 2006 that Europe had simply fallen behind America when it came to funding and ambition.[4]

Resentment

This reach of American economy and culture across the globe is often called "soft power," a term coined by Professor Joseph Nye of Harvard University's John F. Kennedy School of Government. It has become a ubiquitous phrase to describe American influence that is not the result of conscious diplomacy and military power. But "soft power" is an awkward metaphor, deployed to do too much work, from measuring America's moral authority and ability to persuade other countries to do what it wants to simply describing the reach of American culture across the world. Above all, the term does not take into account the very mixed feelings — or outright resentment — the American presence may provoke.

That resentment can trigger opposition to American capitalism — to its opponents' view, the free market at its harshest. An analysis by Stefan Theil, *Newsweek*'s European economics editor, in a study for the German Marshall Fund, noted that in a 2005 poll, just 36 percent of French said that they supported a market economy, and that European school textbooks can be openly hostile to the notion. "Economic growth imposes a hectic form of life, producing overwork, stress, nervous depression, cardiovascular disease, and, according to some, even the development of cancer," declared the *Histoire du XXe Siècle,* a text for high school students preparing for university. Another paper discussed whether technological progress reduces jobs. Theil cited a German social studies text called *FAKT* which blames unemployment on computers and robots, and tells the jobless how to join antireform protest groups "in the tradition of the East German Monday demonstrations," which in 1989 helped begin the process that resulted in a toppling of the Communist government the next year. "It is no surprise that the Continent's schools teach through a left-of-center lens," Theil concluded. "The surprise is the intensity of the antimarket bias."[5]

After a single trader's fraudulent dealing brought huge losses to French bank Société Générale in January 2008, earning him the tag of the "Che Guevara of finance" and a "modern hero" in the French press, the *Economist* magazine noted the "contradictions of France's attitude to capitalism: on the one hand, there is widespread suspicion of the markets; on the other, world-class financial skills."[6] It added, too, that the suspicion could be detected as far back as Honoré de Balzac, the nineteenth-century novelist who wrote, "Behind every great fortune lies a forgotten crime."

That reflex — recoiling from free-market principles as too harsh, as contrary to the principles of European social democracy—has persisted even though the United States' economy has grown faster than most European economies (including those of France and Germany) for the past fifteen years, raising its citizens' living standards and cutting unemployment in ways those European countries would love to emulate.

In recent years, Nicolas Sarkozy, in campaigning to become president of France, and Angela Merkel, in becoming German chancellor, proposed reforms to take their countries toward the "Anglo-Saxon" model, making it easier to hire and fire people, and encouraging competition. Sarkozy was stirred up by a deep sense of national gloom at the stubbornness of unemployment, dragged back below 10 percent only with great pain. In Merkel's case, the motivation came partly from her roots in East Germany, her opposition to socialism and her natural pro-American bent, and an acute consciousness of the struggles for her old compatriots in finding work in a united Germany.

But in each country, the reforms have wilted in the face of protests from labor unions, and in Merkel's case, from coalition partners drawn from the center-left and from a philosophy where mistrust of the markets runs deep. In a phrase that has hung over German corporate and financial policy ever since it was used in April 2005, Vice-Chancellor Franz Müntefering referred to foreign investors as "locusts."[7] The

British press had dubbed Merkel, on her emergence, as "Germany's Margaret Thatcher" — intended as a compliment, out of the conviction that Germany needed a dose of Lady Thatcher's prescriptions even though her legacy remains contentious at home. But Merkel was never going to be a German Thatcher, and she did not even manage to become the chancellor she wanted to be, such was the opposition to her reforms.

In fact, it has been German companies themselves who have managed to push through the changes in deals with their own workers that politicians have failed to accomplish. In 2005, the year when this phenomenon gathered pace, Mercedes pushed through 8,500 job cuts while Volkswagen was able to make large workforce reductions because its union accepted that without these cuts, a plant would close. Changes that were too controversial as German national policy were possible for managers and union bosses sitting across a table.

In Sarkozy's case, once elected, he developed a new refrain that European countries "should not be so naive as to expose our companies to competition," which contradicted his earlier free-market rhetoric.

In backing away from making such market reforms, these French and German politicians are responding to the ambivalence of their own people about America and "American-style capitalism." They want the best of the United States — the scientific discovery, the technological innovation, the anticancer drugs. Quite a few want American music and movies, too — those products were not thrust on foreign audiences against their will. But they criticize or reject the system that produced them.

Anti-Globalization, Anti-American

In this short argument I cannot do justice to the extraordinary tangle of agendas and players in the anti-globalization movement, which has set itself against the opening of trade barriers and which has come to identify the United States — and American companies — as the prime villains. But the movement has been an exercise in such systematic misrepresentation of the benefits of free trade and free markets that it has, through jeopardizing trade talks, done real damage to the interests of the poorest people on the planet, those it says it wants to help.

If there is a single moment when the movement came of age, it was the November 1999 Seattle trade riots, when the cast of a chaotic opera assembled on the streets of that normally serene city. European diplomats, dressed in their uniform of coats with fur collars, Homburg hats, and good leather shoes, tried to pick their way through dreadlocked demonstrators wearing papier-mâché turtle shells. José Bové, a sheep farmer from France's Larzac and a nationally loved figure back home for his campaign against "McDomination," drew thousands to his rallies as he held lumps of Roquefort cheese aloft, with Danielle Mitterrand, wife of the late president, sitting adoringly at his feet.

The opponents of globalization are, as Martin Wolf at the *Financial Times* has written in his superb book on the phenomenon, a mixture of those who have something to lose from the opening of trade barriers — such as labor unions and, in the past, farmers — and a medley of environmental campaigners, nongovernmental organizations, and charities (prominently, Christian Aid) who argue that trade, on terms they believe are set by America, hurts the world's poorest.[8]

It would be foolish to suggest that there are no cases in which free trade makes some people worse off. Paul Collier, a professor of economics at Oxford University who worked for five years at the World Bank, in his passionate analysis of how to rescue the world's poorest countries, particularly those in Africa, argued that rich countries should give them preferential terms of trade if they are in no position yet to compete.[9]

But to take the cause of anti-globalization beyond

those particular cases is a grotesque misrepresentation of the principles of the benefit from trade. As Adam Smith described that benefit in 1776, "If a foreign country can supply us with a commodity cheaper than we ourselves can make it, better buy it of them with some part of the produce of our own industry, employed in a way in which we have some advantage." As advocates of more open markets argue, the lowering of trade barriers helps poor countries. Peter Mandelson, the European Union's trade commissioner, in a February 2008 speech attacking the "backlash" against trade, said that economic integration had "operated as an unprecedented ladder out of poverty," noting that developing countries now account for a third of all global trade.[10]

On the whole, the United States has been firmly on the side of opening up trade, although its presidents have proved easy prey for protectionists in Congress. The Farm Bill, signed in May 2002 by President George W. Bush, who has been otherwise vigorously in favor of free trade, was one of the worst pieces of legislation dreamed up for decades, showering $180 billion in subsidies over ten years on the mere two million people who still run a farm in the United States. In Seattle in 1999, President Bill Clinton delivered a speech guaranteed to scupper the talks, in which he declared his sympathy for the rioters, adding that he was part of the generation which had demonstrated in the 1960s. But Seattle aside, Clinton's instincts did generally come down in favor of trade, and he was justified in saying that trade deals were one of the achievements of which he was proudest.

In general, it is fair to say that the United States' actions have been in line with its philosophy—and that the effects, over the last twenty years, have been to help lift millions of people out of poverty. Without American leadership in this area, that would very likely not have happened.

An Exaggeration of American Power

The railing against American commercial power and cultural reach is often based on exaggerations. In many cases, the power was never as great as critics made it out to be. There are many examples. The 1980s and 1990s were the height of the Coca-Cola Company's reach, under Roberto Goizueta, its legendary chief executive officer. But since the start of the twenty-first century, the company has been struggling to push profits ahead in a more health-conscious market, triggering headlines such as "Why Coca-Cola Has Lost Its Fizz." The company lists competition and consumers' worries about obesity as threats to its markets in developed countries, while warning that "due to product price, limited purchasing power, and cultural differences, there can be no assurance that the company's products will be accepted in any particular developing or emerging market."[11] That is, it's too expensive for the world's poorest, and when you come down to it, they prefer their own.

Similarly, McDonald's, after the heady days of seeing its golden arches opening throughout the former Soviet Union and Red China, found itself battling against health concerns and the spread of coffee chains. Wal-Mart, having tried to push into Europe, found tight planning laws a choke on the kind of superstore it could set up so easily across all of America.

It is possible that America's 2003 invasion of Iraq did even more damage to these iconic brands; commentators were quick to assume that was the case when Coca-Cola's revenues in Europe fell in 2004 and the sales of McDonald's were flat. But the trends which have given such companies trouble go well beyond that single event.

Hollywood

It is worth a particular word about Hollywood, because it has been one of the greatest provocations of resentment against America, as well as one of its most successful exports.

Hollywood's success within the United States and abroad began with its skill at responding to the extraordinary challenge it faced at the start of the twentieth century: trying to appeal to an American audience of immigrants, many not speaking the same language. "These circumstances forced editors, writers, and producers to invent cosmopolitan techniques for reaching out to the largest possible crowd of readers, listeners, and viewers," argued the academics Michael Werz and Barbara Fried in their study of anti-Americanism in 2007. Hollywood, "a community of émigrés," provided "entertainment to an audience that otherwise lacked common traditions or backgrounds, thus serving as a tool of orientation amid the unfamiliar living conditions of the New World."[12]

To dismiss this pursuit as "mass culture," uninterested in subtleties, is to ignore the intelligence of the techniques and Hollywood's importance as a unifying factor in the United States. But in any case, you could not reasonably call it an exercise in trying to dominate the world with a uniform American culture. As Hollywood knew best of all, there was no such thing.

And as Hollywood's investors have been all too aware, its global reach has not been matched by steadiness of profits. For all that critics attack the

"Hollywood formula," there is no such thing as a reliable recipe for a hit. The unpredictability of the winners, the expense of the failures — the studios have had limited success in shielding themselves against these constants from the start. According to *Screen Digest,* the major studios' entire list of 132 films in 2006 was set to lose $1.9 billion over the five-year period when all the revenue from cinemas, television, DVDs, and the Internet would come in.[13] Also the studios, terrified of Internet piracy, have not been sure-footed in exploiting this new medium.

Now, heading toward the same fate as that suffered by other iconic American brands, Hollywood is gradually losing share as other countries realize they prefer their own movies — and can make them, too. For example, India's Bollywood appears finally to be breaking out of the box in which it has been trapped for two decades, making extravaganzas out of singing, dancing, stories of evil landlords and brothers separated at birth — movies which packed cinemas but failed to make much money by international standards. Between 1985 and 2000, its revenues stalled at about $1 billion a year, less than a third of the box office take of a leading Hollywood studio, according to an analysis in *Newsweek.*[14] But more recently, buoyed by the emergence of an Indian middle class and an affluent expatriate audience in Europe and the United

States, Bollywood is producing movies that appeal to the new market.

It would be hard to call Bollywood conservative, given the sexiness of the costumes and the dancing. But all the same, many countries have found that developing their own movies and television shows offers them an escape from what they perceive to be an American wave of loose morality, violence, and materialism bearing down on them.

Declining Influence of the American Media

The same pattern of gradually waning influence is true more generally of the American media, preeminent for most of the twentieth century. As Jeremy Tunstall, a professor of sociology at London's City University, reported in his book *The Media Were American,* the United States and UK in 1948 had 98 percent of the world's television receivers (although U.S. TV sets outnumbered UK ones fourteen to one). The American lead peaked around that same year, particularly in its movies and popular music, in its news magazines such as *Life* and *Time,* and in its news agencies, the AP and the UPA. But after that, while "looking superlative," American media actually began to lose market share, while McCarthyism and then Vietnam chipped away at their moral authority, Tunstall suggests. He also describes how the world outside the United States now devotes only 10 percent of its time to American media; 10 percent to other media imports; and 80 percent to domestic national media.[15] It is astonishing how quickly that change can take place. In Pakistan, President Pervez Musharraf, who seized power in a 1999 military coup but who, as dictators go, was at the relaxed end of the spectrum, allowed private television to start up for the first time, and thirty stations sprang up within six years. The lesson is clear: people prefer products tailored to their own tastes where they can get them.

American Distrust of Big Business

Another oddity of the portrayal of America as the land of uncurbed capitalism is that it ignores America's historical suspicion about the motives of business tycoons. This suspicion has taken a most vigorous and principled form in the antitrust legislation which has underpinned American competitiveness. But it is also reflected in its literature of the early twentieth century, from Theodore Dreiser's *The Financier* in 1912 and *The Titan* in 1914 to Sinclair Lewis's *Babbitt* in 1922. Of course, there are parallels in European literature, but those authors are hardly writing against the grain of their countries' economic organization.

The rigor with which the United States is prepared to deploy its competition policy on its most successful businesses would not be replicated easily in many European countries, which remain highly protective of their own "national champions" (even if entirely happy to join America in attacking Microsoft's market dominance). Europe's politicians profess to believe in the benefits of free trade for both sides, even if one side can make everything more cheaply — but they do not easily shed the instinctive fear that their side will lose out.

The Price the United States Pays for Federalism

A third point missed by the United States' critics is that not everything works well there, and sometimes this is the result of putting its principles of federalism (the respect for states' rights) and its passion for curbing potential monopolies above convenience, progress, and profit. These critics imagine an America in which the pursuit of profit always carries the day, but the picture is much more complex.

Take, for example, the restriction on banking across state borders — or even on banks having branches within one state — which has been in place for most of American history, relaxed only in the last twenty years. The United States, in contrast to most countries, spawned tens of thousands of banks, many of them tiny community ones, but has been slow to develop customer services such as nationwide networks of ATMs and debit cards. Until recently, it was a painful experience to try to persuade a shopkeeper in one state to accept a check from a bank in another.

These regulations, reinforced after the 1929 crash with the 1933 Banking Act, put the ability of even national banks to expand in the hands of state governments. At the same time, the 1933 Glass-Steagall Act separated commercial and investment banking. It was only in 1999 that Congress, after eleven failed attempts at reform in twenty years, finally managed to shed the antiquated laws and take the United States closer to the modern banking regulation it needed.

Banking is the starkest example — given the United States' image as the pinnacle of capitalism — of where America's history and federal structure hamper its economy. But it has handicapped itself in the same way in telecommunications and electricity, two services whose costs affect everyone and every business in the country, and whose regulators have struggled to foster an efficient and competitive industry, and have still partly failed.

In 2001 the world looked on, astonished, as California, whose name is synonymous with sunshine and the good life, imposed the first mandatory power cuts since the Second World War, after households had suffered months of soaring electricity bills. That was the result of deregulating electricity without having increased the supply.

Across the country, more than a decade after the hugely ambitious 1996 Telecommunications Act, which tried to set the terms on which long-distance and local phone companies should deal with each other, competition between telephone companies is still patchy. The United States may have driven the rise of the Internet, but was slow to develop networks of cellular phones and, now, broadband.

The hidden cost of federalism was a theme thoughtfully developed by John Donahue, an associate professor at Harvard University's John F. Kennedy School of Government, in his book *Disunited States,* which argued that competition between the states often hurt the American economy overall. Donahue pointed to the huge amounts of money that states were using to lure businesses — and jobs — across state borders, including, famously, Alabama's successful courtship of Mercedes, counterbidding against almost every state in the South. Alabama's package of subsidies and tax breaks eventually approached $300 million, a cost per job approaching three times the previous record.

In February 2008 the Supreme Court ruled that federal laws should prevail over often tougher state laws aimed at protecting consumers' health and safety, when it barred a suit from a man injured by a heart catheter which had been approved by the Food and Drug Administration. The Court "showed its appreciation for the problem of the Balkanization of the economy by state laws and the difficulties of having to comply with inconsistent state laws in a national economy," said Robin Conrad, executive vice president of the National Chamber Litigation Center, the legal arm of the U.S. Chamber of Commerce.[16]

I don't cite these examples to show that American capitalism does not work; manifestly, it does. But they do show that the United States has often, in industries that are at the heart of its economy, put that pursuit of profit below the principle of states' independence.

Wounded Giant?

Even before the sudden slowing of the American economy in early 2008, the United States' share of the world economy was beginning to shrink. The contribution it makes to the world's overall economic growth is dropping — from 19 percent to just 12 percent in the past decade. The International Monetary Fund expects the world's economic growth to be 4.8 percent in 2008, but within that, the United States will be expanding at less than 2 percent, and the rest of the world together almost three times as quickly. The United States will lose its claim to some of the superlatives (and that was on the cards even before the slowdown of early 2008). It is indeed set to be overtaken by China as the world's biggest economy, although that depends on how you measure size and translate Chinese figures — and as I discuss in chapter 9, those projections rely on a lot of questionable assumptions about China's ability to manage its own growth. Germany is already the world's biggest exporter, despite having an economy less than a quarter the size of the United States'.

But for America, that is neither a source for humiliation nor a reason for gloom. It is easy to exaggerate the potential of China, India, and indeed Asia. For all the uncertainties of the sudden slump in 2008, the proved success of the United States' economic engine is not about suddenly to dissolve. Rather, the quick reaction of the Federal Reserve, in using taxpayers' money to rescue Bear Stearns, Wall Street's fifth-largest bank, shows the poverty of the usual caricature of American capitalism as unbridled, unaided, and unregulated. America is the heart of capitalism, but woven through it is a long, messy history of intervention and regulation.

The pity of critics' resentment of American economic strength is that they regard it as a zero-sum game: as if America's gain is their loss. But it isn't. They do not comfortably acknowledge that the United States could be better off for its innovation, or for the success of its companies, or for its trade — and so could they. That is the hopefulness of American society; it is a shame that this is not one of its more successful exports. The United States has, however, found capital markets easier to promote than its own version of democracy. The next chapter argues that in American foreign policy, the pursuit of democracy is also an admirable goal.

Chapter 5

THE PURSUIT OF
DEMOCRACY

I was in the Karachi villa of a well-connected Pakistani couple on the night of October 19, 2007, just after Benazir Bhutto had returned from exile and a suicide bomber had killed 140 in her homecoming rally. The hosts were unsurpassably cosmopolitan, with museum-quality Islamic and European art on the walls ("Mummy picked it up over the years"), a sophistication compromised only by an impossible request for names of bargain restaurants in Mayfair, London's district of ambassadors and hedge funds.

For all their Western tastes, they maintained an absolute conviction that America had been the perpetrator of the attack, through its agent President Pervez Musharraf and his intelligence services. There was no sense that these accusations might be proved or disproved by forensic analysis (and indeed, the police made little attempt to collect it — then or when Bhutto was later assassinated). It was preferable to assume an obscure purpose; there always had been one, in America's manipulations of Afghanistan and Pakistan, they said.

My Pakistani acquaintances are hardly alone in that preference for conspiracy as the prime technique of explanation. It is suffocatingly common in societies where people cannot readily establish the truth. This is a view of the world which finds incredible the innocence of politics in the West: those wide-eyed speeches in which Tony Blair professed his convictions; Gordon Brown's invocation of his "moral compass"; George W. Bush's declarations that Arabs want democracy, too; or even that disarming technique of State Department officials of explaining their country's foreign policy by projecting a neat list of American aims onto the wall before their audience, the PowerPoint file carried with them in their pockets on a computer thumb drive.

To call America naive in its foreign policy and particularly in its promotion of democracy, as so many have done after Iraq, is not wrong. But it captures only one reason for the gulf between the United States' own vision of its mission to improve the world and the suspicion of critics that America's actions are determined by its own interests and are only coincidentally benign. That is an unfair judgment. This chapter makes three points in defending the broad thrust of American foreign policy, particularly in the last century.

First, America's actions abroad, from its origins up to the Iraq invasion, have been inspired by a complex mixture of imperialism and idealism — a belief in its special mission to export its own values. That can be heavy-handed, but it is also admirable in many ways. Second, it has oscillated between introversion and engagement, and the rest of the world should overwhelmingly prefer America's engagement, through which the United States has helped write international laws and arms control treaties. Third, the promotion of democracy, now mocked for its unforeseen consequences, is the idealistic essence of American policy. The United States' best defense in its recent actions abroad is that it was acting in that honorable cause, and this goal should be salvaged from the icy bath of "realism" that has followed the Iraq debacle.

A Moral Mission

American foreign policy represents a long debate about whether it should intervene abroad or not. In two centuries, it has tried out both answers. In one of the earliest descriptions of the country's intent, John Quincy Adams, then the secretary of state and later the sixth president, in a speech to the House of Representatives, declared, "Wherever the standard of freedom and independence has been or shall be unfurled, there will her heart, her benedictions, and her prayers be. But she goes not abroad, in search of monsters to destroy. She is the well-wisher to the freedom and independence of all. She is the champion and vindicator only of her own."[1]

That is hardly an expression of imperial design. It is easier to find that later, in the 1880s, when America began to emerge as the world's largest economic power. The Spanish-American War of 1898, in which the United States seized Spanish colonies in the Caribbean and the Pacific, marked America's emergence as a world power. In his October 1898 decision to annex all of the Philippines, President William McKinley is reported to have said that God Almighty had ordered him to make the territory an American colony. Senator Albert J. Beveridge of Indiana echoed this in 1900, declaring, "God has not been preparing the English-speaking and Teutonic peoples for a thousand years for nothing but vain and idle self-contemplation and self-admiration....He has made us adept in government that we may administer government among savage and senile peoples."[2]

America's endeavors abroad have long produced a steady supply of such proclamations, although put as baldly as that, they carry an antique air no politician these days would venture. Many critics have argued that this instinct reflects America's Puritan origins — its sense of being divinely anointed to redeem humanity — a case made particularly well by George McKenna, author of *The Puritan Origins of American Patriotism*. McKenna, professor emeritus at the City College of the City University of New York, argues that these convictions have threaded through American foreign policy all the way to the present, and that they inspired America's response to 9/11.[3]

The American exercise of muscle in the Philippines did not go without opposition; it gave rise, among other critics, to the New England Anti-Imperialist League, established in Boston, whose members included Mark Twain and Andrew Carnegie. Rudyard Kipling, in "The White Man's Burden," in 1899, warned that America would not be thanked by the people it had taken on itself to improve.[4] But many others agreed that the United States had all but a duty to press ahead.

Conviction of moral purpose does not guarantee morally admirable behavior, of course; indeed it may convince leaders that they are licensed to suspend such standards in pursuit of their goals. The

Philippine-American War is now compared to Iraq, given the United States' difficulty in putting down a guerrilla movement supported by much of the population, and its resort to torture and burning down villages to do so. Nor does conviction guarantee success: with echoes of President Bush's "Mission Accomplished," President Theodore Roosevelt declared that the Philippine war was over on July 4, 1902, when fighting did not stop for years.

But to deny that this guiding inspiration exists is to misrepresent one of the dominant impulses of American policy. There is much that is admirable about it, including the belief that everyone is entitled to liberty. Those who rush to say that America's foreign intervention is "all about oil" or some other tangible self-interest miss the deep strain of idealism in its motives.

Isolation After the First World War, Engagement After the Second

Having said that, America's willingness to engage with problems outside its borders has ebbed and flowed, the two strongest tides being toward isolation after the First World War and toward deep and painstaking engagement after the Second. There has been much intricate debate about whether America's isolation after the calamity of the Great War contributed to the Great Depression and permitted the rise of fascism. But at least part of the lesson the United States drew from the Second World War was that it would do what it could to prevent a repetition.

That determination gave rise not just to the Marshall Plan, the laborious and expensive reconstruction of Europe, but to the great cornerstones of international institutions, aiming to bring order to international security as well as to the world economy. In those postwar years, America was the driving force behind the creation of the United Nations, the International Monetary Fund, and the World Bank, all in 1945; the North Atlantic Treaty Organization four years later; and the Japanese-American Security Treaty soon after, which helped bring stability to East Asia. It helped draw up the 1970 Nuclear Non-Proliferation Treaty, perhaps the most important of the arms treaties. While the pact has not had complete success in preventing the spread of nuclear weapons, it has been a central reason why the world has managed, for more than sixty years after the American strikes on Nagasaki and Hiroshima, to avoid another use of a nuclear weapon in conflict.

Even though the usefulness of all these institutions is now under challenge by the United States as well as others, that does not negate their stabilizing influence in the aftermath of the Second World War and during the Cold War. True, the United States helped bring them into being in a form which gave it a leading role (and has objected when that role has been challenged, most directly in the United Nations), but it would be wrong to take the next step and call their creation entirely self-serving on America's part and to deny the ideals the United States brought to their creation. The sense of their purpose may be fraying now, but that is not to dismiss their importance — and America's role in bringing that about.

After the Cold War

The end of the Soviet Union freed America from the responsibility for defending European democracies, and with that, its instincts turned inward again. The two post–Cold War presidents, Bill Clinton and George W. Bush, are more similar than the towering drama of Iraq suggests, in their reluctance, in many areas, to get involved with foreign disputes. Both showed an increasing detachment from Europe, including some-times sharp differences of opinion over defense policy and the Middle East. While the events of September 11, the Afghan and Iraq conflicts, and President Bush's conception of a "War on Terror" exacerbated these differences, they were there since the end of the Cold War.

In European eyes, President Clinton's foreign policy is symbolized by Kosovo, the seventy-eight days of aerial bombing in 1999 to halt the "ethnic cleansing" of the Albanian majority of the Serbian province. The NATO assault depended crucially on American airpower, but President Clinton was still denounced by many in Europe for fighting a "cowardly war," refusing to risk American servicemen's lives. The question is why America became involved at all. In Pentagon presentations at the time, Kosovo, on the southern fringe of Europe, seemed a world away, with its ironwork balconies, people with wedge-shaped Slavic faces, and thousand-year-old rivalries.

Part of the answer to why the United States became involved was President Clinton's personal propensity to see in divided communities — Kosovo, Northern Ireland, the Middle East — a problem that he felt should be resolvable through better communication. He was prone to spot in these far-off conflicts a parallel with the American enterprise of uniting people who might otherwise have good reason not to get along. It was sometimes an inappropriate projection, and it arguably led him to embrace pet schemes to which the United States could devote attention — and many words — without the risk of military casualties. Those efforts also proved a distraction from the greater problem of helping Russia build a stable civic society, a task the United States would dearly have liked to off-load onto Europe but could not, and for which the opportunity is now past.

The Clinton years offered a portrait of evasion, with carefully chosen exercises in foreign enthusiasm. The United States did insist on its own terms in its engagement, but if this was imperialism, it was of a reluctant kind. Europe, which did not distinguish itself over Kosovo other than by immobility, should count itself lucky that Bill Clinton chose to get involved at all.

September 11 Reawakened America's Sense of Mission

In the eight months before the attacks, President Bush had shown little inclination to be active abroad and little familiarity with Europe or the Middle East. His gaffe-prone tour of Europe in June 2001 met with protests (over climate change and missile defense) and headlines mocking his apparent ignorance, such as "Bush Renames Spanish Prime Minister" (he called José María Aznar, "Anzar") and "Bush Meets Royalty, Ignores Reality."

Three months later came the attacks that have been called the most traumatic event on American soil since Pearl Harbor. They provoked not just the invasion of Afghanistan but, as President Bush put it in his State of the Union speech of January 2002, the condemnation of an "axis of evil" of Iraq, Iran, and North Korea. In that leap, the logic of which remains opaque, President Bush set America not just on the path to war with Saddam Hussein but on a mission to export democracy to the greater Middle East.

I shall discuss in later chapters why America so badly misjudged those challenges, the practical problems it now faces as a result, and also its indefensible actions — those areas where it will have to work to regain a claim to morality. But the point I want to make here is that in his response to 9/11, President Bush was not acting at odds with the enduring spirit of American policy, even if it marked a change from President Clinton's discursive style. September 11 reawakened America's recurrent historic sense of mission about reforming the world in its image.

As Thomas Donnelly, a resident fellow at the right-wing American Enterprise Institute in Washington, DC, puts it, there is a "set of predilections, tendencies, visions, myths, fallacies, traditions, and experiences that has led Americans to make choices in international politics that others might not and which, taken together, form a remarkably consistent approach to making policy and, especially, to using armed force."[5] That is not to justify President Bush's decisions in Iraq, but it is to put them in a long tradition of similarly motivated impulses. Many of these impulses have driven the most beneficial actions in American foreign policy—and will very likely continue to do so.

The Mistaken "War on Terror"

The misconceived "War on Terror," the first of President Bush's two great themes in foreign policy, was not one of those admirable reflexes. You might ask what damage the mere choice of words can do; the answer is, a lot. By defining the pursuit of radical Islamists as a war, Bush made it impossible for America to identify its enemies. The language conflates all kinds of terrorist groups and causes—many of them stubbornly local and territorial in their obsessions: Kashmir, Chechnya, and Palestine, to name just three. Al Qaeda is the rarity in having an aspiration—the restoration of the old Islamic caliphate—that extends across continents. The notion that America was at war made it easy for Bush to make the unjustified leap from retaliation for 9/11 to the invasion of Iraq.

The phrase "War on Terror" also leads to a disastrous strategy: you cannot define success, other than by the absence of attack, or know that the war has ended (one of the sources of the legal mess into which the United States has cast itself in Guantánamo Bay). And the metaphor of "war" threads every policy with belligerence, implying that force is the only appropriate tool (and it will be very hard for Bush's successors to drop that language, for fear of being accused of going soft on terror). The phrase also alienates America from European countries with large Muslim populations which should be its allies.

Promotion of Democracy

But if the "War on Terror" is the worst of President Bush's big themes, the promotion of democracy is among the better ones, although now derided. It has been a constant theme of modern American presidents, as well as those in the eighteenth and nineteenth centuries. John F. Kennedy, in his inaugural speech in January 1961, declared, "Let every nation know, whether it wishes us well or ill, that we shall pay any price, bear any burden, meet any hardship, support any friend, oppose any foe, to assure the survival and the success of liberty."

Less lyrically, George W. Bush, in the 2006 National Security Strategy, announced that "It is the policy of the United States to seek and support democratic movements and institutions in every nation and culture, with the ultimate goal of ending tyranny in our world," a phrase that reached so hard for resonance, it could have come from the script of *Star Trek*. More practically, he argued that "The goal of our statecraft is to help create a world of democratic, well-governed states that can meet the needs of their citizens and conduct themselves responsibly in the international system. This is the best way to provide enduring security for the American people."[6]

That last claim—about improving American security—is a bold one which can be judged only over decades. There are reasons to think it might hold good over generations, but it is hard to count on it producing American allies tomorrow. It relies on the principle that democracies are more loath than are other forms of government to go to war, and are more able to defuse grievances that would otherwise be expressed violently. But as the United States has found in Iraq, Lebanon, and the Palestinian territories, when people are newly free to choose their leaders, they may choose ones who particularly dislike the American giant. If people are very worried about security, they will choose authoritarian leaders (as Russians arguably did in repeatedly backing Vladimir Putin for president, although the minuscule choice of alternative candidates offered to voters hardly counts as democracy). If they are enraged by corruption and inequality, they may be lured by religious firebrands.

But while it is not a law of nature, the incentive for people eventually to pick leaders who strengthen democracy and encourage capital markets is clear, in the improvement in their own lives which that promises. President Bush would have found it simpler to defend the pursuit of democracy by saying bluntly that it is the system which most accommodates people's dignity, and that they want it, as Iraqis, Afghans, Kenyans, and people in western Pakistan showed in running huge risks to vote. He was at his rare best when he argued that point.

The United States deserves part of the credit for what has now been three decades of democracy spreading around the world, including in Latin America (apart from Cuba). In the 1970s, Portugal, Greece, and Spain shook off authoritarian regimes; more recently, so did South Korea, Taiwan, Indonesia, the Philippines, and much of Africa. The most dramatic changes have been in Central and Eastern Europe, where ten countries which had been part of the Soviet bloc joined the European Union in barely a decade and a half. True, the trend has not been one-way. The "color revolutions"—such as the Orange Revolution in Ukraine and the Rose Revolution in Georgia—are fading; the Central Asian "stans," of which the United States had such high hopes, are a collection of autocracies; in Thailand, generals are in power more than a year after a coup against an elected leader. As Niall Ferguson, the historian, has argued, "Only slowly, by sometimes painful trial and error, do elites learn that it is in their own interests to exclude violence from politics, to take turns at governing, and above all to submit to the rule of law."[7]

But that does not mean that nothing can be done to encourage efforts toward democracy. The United States has worked hard to support countries who make such moves, in offering to trade more openly with them, in extending membership of NATO to some, and in encouraging the European Union to take them in, too. Despite the hazards of trying to spread democracy, the list of horrors in American foreign policy is notable more for the times when the United States departed from the pursuit of democracy than for those where it pursued it to the point of disastrous success, as in Iraq. The long obsession with the defeat of Communism inspired the misjudgments of Vietnam. The horrors of the regimes which the United States backed in Central America, undermining popular leaders in favor of those it believed would resist Communism, have been well chronicled.[8]

More recently, in Pakistan, the United States was mistaken in wholeheartedly backing the military regime of President Pervez Musharraf, believing he could best help in the pursuit of Al Qaeda and the Taliban. It overlooked the extent to which the military was becoming the problem in Pakistan, not the solution, sucking up funds which would better have been spent on education — in a country where half the people can't read — and building up resentment in the poorer provinces. The inevitable end to President Musharraf's tenure as a military leader was the democratic elections of 2008, the only means of defusing the explosive anger against his rule. That is a lesson against too much realism — against the kind of pragmatism the Bush administration argued was justified by the "War on Terror."

Of course, the pursuit of democracy has to be tempered by other concerns, such as stability. The United States is understandably muted now in talking of democracy in Egypt, Saudi Arabia, and Central Asia, worried about energy supplies and combating terrorism. But as Pakistan has shown, backing military dictators is not a recipe for long-term peace; it may instead inflame the terrorism which the dictators have promised to quash.

I have argued in this chapter that the United States has made an enormous contribution to world security and order, and to the spread of democracy. I shall argue in the next chapter that those who accuse it, after Iraq, of no longer upholding those principles are wrong.

Chapter 6

ARROGANT BUT NOT LAWLESS

One of the most important accusations against the United States in the wake of Iraq is that it refuses to recognize international law if it does not suit its purposes. The charge is that America has violated its own principles, showing itself uninterested in upholding the international order it spent half a century working to construct. It needs to reclaim that moral authority to justify future international pressure, military or diplomatic. As one British minister put it, "There is a case for liberal intervention after the temple of Iraq came crashing down, but it has to be Iraq-with-rules."[1]

America has always had a different attitude toward international laws and institutions than smaller countries, which stems not just from its size but its

Constitution and its belief that it is making its own laws, independent of other countries. But I argue that America's dismissive attitude toward international law in the Iraq invasion does not mean that it has to surrender its overall claim that it works with other countries under the international laws and institutions it helped build. The list of ways in which the United States is seen to dismiss such laws and treaties is often hurled at it in one melded block, as if there is no distinction between the supposed offenses. The United States' best defense is that it is picking and choosing among these institutions; that some of them are showing the strain of trying to fit a world radically changed in the half century since they came into being; and that, since Iraq, it is trying harder to work within these principles. It has a strong case, although one that, after Iraq and Guantánamo, it needs to strengthen further.

Arrogance and the Bush Administration

The accusation that America is now entirely indifferent to international laws and institutions is provoked largely by a series of decisions by the United States during the presidency of George W. Bush, of which the invasion of Iraq in 2003 is the most controversial. These include the decision to quit the 1972 Anti-Ballistic Missile Treaty in 2002, a casual approach to the Nuclear Non-Proliferation Treaty, the continued refusal to ratify the Kyoto Protocol on climate change, the refusal to recognize the International Criminal Court, and a general contempt for the United Nations.

In addition, although the United States has traditionally kept trade disputes separate from diplomacy, the Bush administration approved a farm bill of such extravagant subsidies to farmers that it jeopardized the Doha trade round, a hugely ambitious attempt to write a new global trade pact particularly aimed at helping some of the poorest countries. President Bush's keenness to pass a new farm bill in the final months of his tenure also threatened Doha, as did his enthusiasm for one-on-one deals with other countries—seen by economists and trade negotiators as a threat to the ambitious but precarious structure of broader global trade deals.

Other provocations included using the traditional American prerogative to name the head of the World Bank to put into that position Paul Wolfowitz, Donald Rumsfeld's deputy at the Pentagon during the Iraq invasion and one of the most vocal advocates of the war. A further sting was the appointment of John Bolton, again one of the most abrasive figures of the war, as the United States' ambassador to the United

Nations. He was never a conciliator; the *Washington Post,* in a rare sortie into wit, said he had failed even to "broker a compromise between his sand-colored mop [of hair] and his snow-colored mustache."[2] Bolton's skepticism toward the United Nations was summed up for many in his declaration in a 1994 speech that "there is no such thing as the United Nations. There is only the international community, which can only be led by the remaining superpower, which is the United States."[3]

It was that arrogant tone, on top of actual decisions, which caused offense among the United States' potential allies, never mind its enemies. There is no question that the Bush administration was egregiously dismissive in its comments about international cooperation, its officials taking apparent delight in offending any country or organization which might presume to count on American support or assume that the United States would work within the established rules. But even though the tone was high-handed, in many disputes, the United States had a fair point.

The Military Burden

The United States' strongest case overall to be upholding international institutions is perhaps its continuing acceptance of its role as "the world's policeman," even though the Cold War has ended. That includes its acceptance of the lion's share of NATO's responsibilities even though the circumstances which prompted the creation of the alliance are gone.

To some extent, the sheer amount of money America spends on its military will give it the role of the world's policeman in any crisis, unless it bluntly refuses to take it up. Even before Iraq, the United States spent more on defense than the next ten countries combined, but that war has taken the discrepancy to even greater heights. In February 2008, President Bush asked Congress for $515 billion, and analysts reckon that 2009 could see outlays of $675 billion—depending on how many troops are kept in Iraq—which would take up 4.4 percent of the U.S. gross domestic product. In comparison, Britain spends about £25 billion ($50 billion) a year on defense—about 2.5 percent of its economy—in turn, a much higher proportion than in continental Europe.

In Afghanistan, a NATO-led effort, the United States still supplies half of the development aid, three-quarters of the military contribution, and 85 percent of the airpower. And it has complained about it; at the start of 2008, Robert Gates, secretary of defense, attacked European allies for not sending more troops. On this point, he is not on the strongest ground, for all the righteousness with which he expressed it. After September 11, NATO members responded, as they were obliged to under the alliance's Article 5, which mandates a commitment to assist another member under attack. Yet the Afghan mission has broadened from the pursuit of Osama bin Laden into setting up all the institutions of state for one of the world's poorest countries — a much more difficult task, and not clearly under the original mandate.

It is understandable that European governments, which do not consider themselves as directly under threat from Afghanistan as does the United States, have not responded as vigorously. (It also seems particularly perverse to berate the German government for keeping its soldiers out of fierce fighting — a stance the German public firmly supports — when America and Europe spent half a century persuading Germany to excise its military reflexes.)

But as a general lament about NATO, the United States has a good case in arguing that Europe should not take the American contribution for granted, and should pay more of the cost for battles close to home.

The United Nations

The United States also has good grounds for some of its frustration with the United Nations, two words that send conservative Americans into a frenzy of exasperation, although the Bush administration went too far in its rejection of the principle of searching for common ground with other countries.

There is a long history behind the United States' irritation, reflected in its intermittent refusal to pay its dues to the United Nations (where it is the largest contributor). It certainly has a good reason to object to the actions of the General Assembly, the only UN body in which every one of the 192 member countries has an equal voice, and which sets the budget, makes resolutions, and appoints temporary members of the Security Council. It is one of the few arenas in which tiny countries can snub the superpower, and they take full advantage of it.

In many of these countries, politicians find it so valuable to be seen to challenge America that their opposition to American initiatives in the United Nations is almost automatic. More than two-thirds of the members of the General Assembly are developing countries, and for the past twenty years, they have made north-south relations the dominant theme of debates. Their anti-American reflexes can lead to absurdity. In the 2006 vote against the deployment of weapons in space, which America lost by 160 votes to 1, many piled on against the superpower even though they had no direct interest or capability in space, a swipe that cost them nothing. The United States is also right to have dismissed as a politicized insult the vote in 2001 which threw it off the United Nations Commission on Human Rights (whose members included such champions of human rights as China, Saudi Arabia, and Russia). At the same time, again by countries eager to score points, America was voted off the International Narcotics Board by a subsidiary council of the assembly.

The rise of the giants of the developing world — China, India, and Brazil — and their desire to express their new strength has moved the center of gravity farther away from the United States. They argue that the structure of the United Nations (including the site of its headquarters in New York) and the small size of the Security Council, where the only permanent members are those who had nuclear weapons soon after the end of World War II, are now out of date. They are right, and the United States would be wrong to think that the United Nations will ever return to the coziness of its first few decades, when the United States' supremacy was unchallenged. But at the same time, the new voices have added to the anti-American tilt of the General Assembly in a way that vindicates the United States' sense that it has become the target of wild political gestures.

The United Nations Security Council

The United States is on weaker ground in its impatience with the Security Council, especially in the run-up to the Iraq invasion. The 1945 Charter of the United Nations, signed by every member country, says that countries have the right to take up arms in self-defense, but that any military action beyond that must be taken only with the authorization of the Security Council. That text, of which the United States was one of the prime authors in the wake of the Second World War, makes the council the cornerstone of any justification for war.

The United States has an entirely fair point that the present structure and powers of the council present real problems in exercising that principle. Any one of the five permanent members — the United States, Russia, China, Britain, and France — can veto a resolution authorizing military action, for whatever its own motives, however strong the support among other countries for action might be. American officials are eloquent in arguing that they should not be hostage to the self-interest of the other four, which only by coincidence will align with their own.

The strength of that argument has been recognized

in the past, albeit in a very few instances. In 1950, when Communist North Korea invaded South Korea, the Security Council did authorize military action against the North. Yet that agreement was achieved only because of two diplomatic accidents: the Soviet Union (a sure veto) was boycotting the council for unrelated reasons, and China's seat was then still held by the Taiwan-based former regime, which was bitterly opposed to Communism. That said, anger among many countries at the invasion was so deep that there was a widespread feeling that the action would have been legitimate even if there had been a veto.

In 1999, the United States and other leading NATO countries did not attempt to get a Security Council resolution authorizing action to stop Slobodan Milošević, Serbia's president, from murdering and expelling Kosovo's ethnic majority of Albanians. They reckoned that Russia would veto it out of sympathy for Serbia, and that China might, too, out of a general dislike for ethnic separatists who rebelled against their sovereign capitals. But again, widespread support, particularly from nearby countries, helped the NATO expedition to claim to be fighting a justified war.

A year and a half later, in the Afghanistan invasion that began on October 7, 2001, the United States did have the council's backing; it unanimously condemned the attacks of September 11 and recognized "the inherent right of individual or collective self-defense." Resolution 1368 passed by the council was not an explicit authorization to use force, but it put no obstacles in its way.

But for Iraq, the United States failed to get a resolution explicitly authorizing the action, nor did it get the widespread support that would have enabled it to argue that it was acting in any case with the goodwill of the international community. The "coalition of the willing" stapled together by the United States included countries peripheral to the conflict, such as El Salvador and Singapore, that were prompted, many thought, mainly by the preferential trade deals they expected to receive from the United States.[4]

The United States never put as much weight on the legality of the action under international law as did Tony Blair, faced with passionate opposition from within his own party in the House of Commons. But to the extent that the United States made a formal case, it was based on the claim that Saddam Hussein was developing weapons of mass destruction, in breach of United Nations prohibitions. As well as relying on intelligence now shown to be false, this argument relied on the doctrine of preemptive war — striking an enemy before it strikes — now part of the U.S. National Security Strategy, but one about which other countries are understandably queasy.

Having failed to get the second resolution, the United States and Britain rested their case that the war was legal all the same on Saddam's breach of United Nations sanctions, and on the "combined effects" of three earlier Security Council resolutions, 678, 687, and 1441, ordering Iraq out of Kuwait and forbidding it from acquiring weapons. As a practical argument, this had some force: the sanctions were unraveling as Russia and other countries sought ways of trading with Iraq. But as a legal argument, it was flimsy. American officials added horror stories about Saddam's brutality, but as a legal justification for urgent military action, such claims would have had real force only in the late 1980s, when he had murdered Kurdish villagers, and again after the 1991 war, when he attacked those who had risen up against him.

The reason Iraq has been so destructive for America's reputation abroad is not just that the mission went wrong, but that the United States dismissed international laws and opinions in pursuing it. In its final two years, the Bush administration appeared to find more use for the Security Council and more value in international support. It used the council as one avenue through which to put pressure on Iran to curb its nuclear ambitions, working with Britain and France within the council to try to get tougher resolutions despite the reluctance of Russia and China. It also turned to the council to rally international help on Sudan.

The United States is right that in many cases winning the unanimous backing of the Security Council will be impossible. The old problem is getting worse. Russia, under President Vladimir Putin, is increasingly hostile in relations with the West; China, while amending its traditional reluctance to take an active role on the world stage, has a keen eye for the allegiances it needs to secure energy supplies. But the United States would be wrong, both in principle and in its own interests, to attribute no value at all to the pursuit of international support and to the success of winning over some allies, even if not all.

Arms Treaties

Given the United States' concerns about Iran, it is disappointing that it has not worked more consistently within the United Nations on proliferation of nuclear weapons, where it helped draw up one of the world's most important arms control pacts, the 1970 Nuclear Non-Proliferation Treaty. The treaty restricted the possession of nuclear weapons to five countries: the United States, the Soviet Union (now Russia), China, Britain, and France. It offered other signatories, in return for not equipping themselves with these weapons, help with the peaceful use of nuclear energy and radioactive material. The United States played an irreplaceable part not just in bringing the treaty to life, but in making the bargain worthwhile for countries which might have been tempted to make a dash for the bomb. It offered them trade and extended over some of them its own security umbrella.

The United States' most damaging action toward the nuclear treaty, in 2006, was to offer India a nuclear cooperation pact that promised enormous help with civil nuclear work. It demanded far too little reassurance that this would not also help India's weapons program, and it seemed to reward a country that had always refused to sign the non-proliferation treaty. But the United States would be justified in arguing that the current fragility of the treaty cannot be blamed on that action; it reflects the weakening of the original "bargain," as countries' desire to get nuclear weapons increases and as it gets easier to do so. That bargain will have to be redrawn if the pact is to hold, and in early attempts to explore whether that is possible, the United States has played a central role.

The United States has also only a partial defense for its decision to leave one of the main arms treaties it struck with the Soviet Union during the Cold War, and then to protest when Russia later made a similar move. The United States said that it had to quit the Anti-Ballistic Missile Treaty in order to develop its controversial missile defense system, or "Star Wars," even though there was no assurance that the huge technical difficulties could be overcome. Yet in 2007, when Russia notified other signatories that it intended to suspend participation in the 1990 Treaty on Conventional Armed Forces in Europe, there was uproar from the Americans.

The treaty, signed in the last days of the Cold War, between NATO and the Warsaw Pact, limited the armed forces and weapons the United States and the former Soviet Union countries could have in Europe. Russia's decision to leave, it said, was in retaliation for America's decision to put new missile bases in Poland and the Czech Republic. There is no question that Russia, under President Putin, took easy offense at such actions, but the United States had lost the high ground by its earlier action. America is right that these treaties are creaking, but it should not cast aside the products of its own efforts too lightly.

International Criminal Court

The United States is on stronger ground in its refusal to recognize the International Criminal Court, although it has conducted its attacks on the court with such hostility that it gives ammunition to those who argue that it is uninterested in any principles of international law.

The court, first conceived by the United Nations in 1948 after the Nuremberg and Tokyo tribunals, to try crimes of war, formally came into being only in 2002. The principle that there should be such trials is an honorable one, and those who oppose it are never going to seem heroic. But the United States has a good case that the court is inevitably open to accusations of arbitrariness, and to partiality, in its selection of cases, given how few cases it will actually try and the huge political resonance each will carry. The United States has a point, too, in arguing that its soldiers are in danger of being singled out for alleged war crimes, given the widespread antipathy in parts of the world to the United States and the desire to see it "brought to book" for alleged offenses.

But it has made a poor job of justifying its objections. Instead, it conveys the sense that no one will hold its soldiers to account except American military courts—if then. When confronted with the evidence of the abuses at Abu Ghraib in Iraq, where American soldiers degraded and abused Iraqi prisoners, the Bush administration dealt with it slowly and with secrecy. The process did not help the credibility of the verdict, which blamed a few junior soldiers acting on their own, an account that remains deeply implausible.

When a British soldier in Iraq was killed in 2003 by American "friendly fire" from an aircraft above, the Pentagon refused for four years to release the cockpit recordings to the family. They were eventually leaked in early 2007 to *The Sun* newspaper in Britain. There was an uproar in Britain, but the reaction of Pentagon officials privately was to say that they should never have shared the information with the British Ministry of Defence, which they suspected of leaking the tape.[5]

This attitude of the United States — that its soldiers are beyond criticism other than its own, in private, at home — gives it a reputation for lawlessness and undermines acceptance of its role as the global policeman. It might feel resentful and complain that others should carry more of the burden, but to the extent that it does act in that role, it presumably wants acceptance and respect.

The Green Villain

The environment is the issue, of those on this list, that is going to give America the most trouble, because it resonates with ordinary people in so many countries. The United States does not easily see itself as the villain of the world's environment, as so many others do. Americans look around and see a green and fruitful land, less polluted, less spoiled, and less populated than many areas of Europe or Asia, and they have a point.

The problem is climate change. America emits more greenhouse gases per person than any other country in the world. Until it was overtaken by China (roughly at the end of 2007), it emitted more than any other country overall, even though its population is just a quarter of China's. That underpins its reputation as greedy, consuming "more than its share" of the world's resources, its people refusing to compromise the world's highest standard of living to save those in poor countries from the effects of climate change. The cars two feet longer than anything you could park in London or Paris, the sport-utility vehicles managing only fourteen miles to the gallon, the huge houses and ferocious air-conditioning — all these are brandished as evidence of America's moral failing. (Although critics never adjust for the smaller size of the American gallon, only 83 percent of the size of the Imperial gallon used in Britain.)

Because of climate change the environment is not America's strongest front. But there are still many points that can be made in its defense that are lost among the insults.

The first is the depth of the environmental tradition in American culture. The American reverence for the wilderness goes back before even the explorers who pushed the frontier westward — back to Native American culture. Robert Hughes, the Australian-born critic known for his historical analysis of his native country and of American art since its origins, has described how early Australian settlers pushed into the interior and found desert, whereas the Americans found a land of plenty. That reinforced Americans' sense of "manifest destiny" — of their special mission — and also their delight in their new territory. German immigrants to America at the end of the nineteenth century added their own strong flavor to the cultural mixture with their particular love of forests and nature.

The Sierra Club, founded in 1892, is one of the world's oldest environmental clubs, now with 1.3 million supporters. When I was a child at school in Washington, DC, in the 1970s, the curriculum was threaded with lectures about recycling and protecting wildlife, a good couple of decades before that became standard in British schools. "It was America which put environmentalism on the world's agenda in the 1970s and 1980s," recalled Glenn Prickett, a senior vice president for Conservation International. "But since then, somehow, the wealthiest and most powerful country on the planet has gone to the back of the line."[6]

A second point in the United States' favor is that the environmental laws it passed in those decades are some of the world's toughest. The 1980 Superfund act (formally known as the Comprehensive Environmental Response, Compensation, and Liability Act), a tax on petroleum and chemical industries to pay for cleaning up toxic land, and the five separate Clean Air acts between 1963 and 1990 were very expensive for American businesses and state governments. So was the drive to tighten health regulations, such as the 1980s move to ban and phase out asbestos. It is a measure of the importance legislators attached to the issue that they were made national standards, not left to states' discretion.

The United States also moved quickly, when a 1976 National Academy of Sciences report found damage to the ozone layer, to ban chlorofluorocarbons from aerosols. It was one of the driving forces behind the 1987 Montreal Protocol to ban substances damaging to the ozone layer and develop replacement technologies, a move resisted initially by the European Union.

What is more, the United States enforces these laws, even if their application is challenged in court. The folly of Lloyd's of London, the three-hundred-year-old insurance market, in thinking that insurance against these costs could be secured against the private wealth and property of the British middle classes was a misjudgment that brought parts of the market to collapse in the late 1980s. But it may have stemmed from a failure to appreciate that in the United States, once a law has been passed, it is generally enforced.

In contrast, although the European Union has been prolific in passing ambitious regulations on environmental standards, the marvel is how patchily they are enforced. Drinking-water standards, cleanliness of beaches, the protection of wildlife habitats — the European Commission in Brussels has had plenty to say on all of these. But the countries on Europe's southern fringe, Greece, Italy, Spain, Portugal — the poorer ones, before the influx of those from the former Soviet bloc — have often been treated with some lenience when they have failed to comply.

Even in France, one of the founders of the European Union and one of its richest countries, compliance has been patchy. The left-wing government of Lionel Jospin between 1997 and 2002 struggled to impose an "eco-tax," to eliminate nitrates from drinking water (a particularly troublesome consequence of farming), and to comply with the toughest measures of the Kyoto accords on climate change, even though he had Green Party members among his ministers.

But then we come to climate change, and America has a more difficult case to make, one that, so far, has won no worldwide sympathy. The Bush administration did, in February 2008, say for the first time that the United States would agree to be bound by limits on emissions — but only if China and India were, too. But that sidesteps their main objection: that the emissions of the developed world have caused the problem and that rich countries should bear the cost of mitigating climate change.

The United States' best defense is that it would find it much more expensive than would other countries to make those changes to its economy, and if it did so abruptly, it would have an effect on growth that would also hurt other economies, particularly the poorest. Given its size, and its reliance on road transport, America is inevitably more dependent on gasoline than are smaller, more densely inhabited countries.

America might add to that another argument (one I'm sympathetic to, even though I'm conscious that it drives my greenest colleagues to a point beyond anger), that there is a moral value in encouraging people's mobility because it encourages their understanding of one another and their ability to work together. Americans' delight in crisscrossing their own country springs from the exhilaration of the American project itself, even though it does carry a cost in pollution.

There is some force in America's defense of its difference from other countries. The Kyoto Protocol, which sets targets for reducing emissions or requires countries to trade permits for them if they exceed the set levels, was much easier for European countries to meet, as it coincided with a shift from coal- to gas-fired power stations, which immediately reduced emissions. Germany was helped by the closure of many old, dirty East German industries, which scythed through the emissions levels of a united Germany, as well as by the slow shrinkage of its aging population. Even given those advantages, the European Union has not found it easy to make the required cuts. The European Environment Agency, a Copenhagen-based think tank, warned in November 2007 that the fifteen European countries covered by the Kyoto commitment (not including those who joined the European Union since 2004) were on course to achieve only a 4 percent cut in emissions, not the 8 percent required.

The United States' proposal to research new green technologies and to export or give them to other countries is also a strong point in its favor. The speed with which it did this with ozone-damaging chemicals was dramatic, although the demands of innovation were less, as substitutes were developed with comparative ease once the need was clear. In December 2007, Bush signed into law new rules on energy efficiency in cars and houses — the Energy Independence and Security Act — which had overwhelming bipartisan support in

Congress. That will slowly but profoundly shift Americans toward cars and appliances that use less fuel.

It is also fair for the Bush administration—and the Clinton administration before it—to claim that there is no point in the president's signing on to curbs that Congress will never pass. A Russian president can push through a law on a whim, but the leader of a democracy cannot, let alone one with the separation of powers dictated by the U.S. Constitution. To that extent, President Bush could be said merely to have been honest in pointing out to the world, at the start of his presidency, that Congress would not pass the Kyoto Protocol, a blunt declaration that President Clinton had avoided making.

However, the weakness of America's case, under Clinton as well as Bush, is that administrations have not tried harder to persuade Congress to back reforms—ones better designed than the Kyoto Protocol, say—building on the significant minority that wants change. The United States could have been much more vigorous, for example, in investigating market-based ways to curb emissions.

It helps the United States' case that, as well as new federal efforts, some of the states have begun moving on their own to encourage behavior that would reduce carbon emissions. That contradicts the caricature of

America as a country unified in its lack of concern about global warming.

The same phenomenon is true in all developed countries—people are concerned about global environmental problems but do not much want to sacrifice their own standard of living to help. It is unfair for countries that, because of the structure of their economy, find these changes easy, to accuse America of entirely neglecting something that it would find more difficult.

Trade: The United States Has Largely Worked Within the Rules

If climate change is one of America's more vulnerable flanks, its promotion of trade liberalization is one of its strongest. The World Trade Organization is perhaps the single international institution and set of rules for which the United States finds the most use. At least it finds the WTO useful as a court—in many years the United States takes more disputes there for resolution than other countries. Like every other country on the planet, it finds the treaty-making side of the organization harder to work with—as the process of trying to write deals demands repeated concessions on all sides.

America's behavior has hardly been perfect. Nor are candidates for Congress or the presidency in an election year the best test of America's free-trade impulses; if you took their torrent of promises to protect American jobs at face value, then the United States would be an island, with nothing bought or sold over its borders.

But to say that America's instincts are overwhelmingly in the direction of liberalizing trade is fair. President George W. Bush's repeated defense of that principle is one of his few unambiguously useful legacies, for the United States and other countries.

Conclusion

The United States has undeniably been high-handed in its approach to international law, an inclination present from its creation. This was flamboyantly the case under the administration of George W. Bush, at least until the worsening situation in Iraq left it chastened.

But Bush's skepticism was a continuation of the approach taken by President Clinton's administration—in Kosovo, in some trade talks—if wildly more abrasive in tone. It was perhaps an inevitable result of the United States' position as the sole superpower and its growing frustration with increasingly strained postwar institutions. Its attitude of "picking and choosing" among those institutions is often justified. They have not all worn well, and while many clearly need reform — the United Nations, some of the arms treaties, and the International Monetary Fund, to name just a few — it is a task so formidable it may be impossible.

That frustration does not make America a lawless nation. Indeed, it is hard to portray a country so imbued with laws — and lawyers — as contemptuous of the discipline, let alone one which has played such a central part in creating the rules and institutions that have helped run the world for half a century. Iraq does not destroy that claim, because there are so many other instances when the United States can argue that it does respect those principles, but it is in its interests to show that it is still committed to that cause.

Chapter 7

THE IRAQ INVASION: STUPID BUT NOT MALIGN

The mess in which America finds itself in Iraq, more than five years after the invasion, has been one of the provocations for this book. The United States' reputation for military supremacy has disintegrated. Its foreign policy is in confusion, beset with a horrendous list of problems, many connected to Iraq. Most of all, America threw away its reputation for competence and judgment, and, for many, its claim to be acting to improve the world. Its enemies are delighted, its allies bewildered.

The questions now are whether anything can be said to redeem the invasion and how much America should be judged by this debacle. Should its future efforts abroad—and its ideology of exporting democracy—be condemned because of its breathtaking mistakes in Iraq?

There are a few points in America's favor, although I am not going to defend either the conception or execution of the war overall. I have never been one of its dogmatic opponents. In the run-up to the war, I was in the camp of those willing to be persuaded, but by the time of the invasion, had not been, skeptical of the urgency and objecting to the lack of international support. But whatever one's view then, the years since have revealed an ugly drama of ideology, wishful thinking, and outright duplicity on the part of the administration. In the United States' record in Iraq, there is little defense against the charges of arrogance, naïveté, deliberate suppression of inconvenient facts, and indifference to the need to justify the action. There is no way to commend America for an invasion that led to the deaths of probably hundreds of thousands of Iraqis and the displacement of millions, as well as the deaths of more than four thousand American soldiers.

It is possible that Iraq may yet "come right" in the brutal sense of being relatively stable and not a cause of turmoil to its neighbors, although there are plenty of signs that it will remain a hideous and dangerous place for those not on the winning side of its countless sectarian divisions. Even if it does improve, America will hardly be able to take credit for a transformation so out of control and at such cost.

Yet there are still some arguments in America's defense (even if each one is ringed around with deep qualifications). It did get rid of a dictator who had killed many of his own people, and promotion of democracy is in itself an honorable aim, although the United States entirely failed to understand how the hatred among Iraq's different groups might make such a transition tremendously difficult, if not impossible.

America can also argue that recent experience has already changed it and strengthened its own democracy. Bush's successors will take care to sound very different on such themes. Congress (and the media) are now reminded of their role in challenging the president. The intelligence agencies are strengthened in their ability to defend their own findings against the administration. The army has been converted to the need to be good at peace building as well as fighting, a shift that will make American policy far more versatile. Americans themselves will take less on faith from their leaders.

However, America will be judged most on how it behaves in Iraq and the region. It will find it hard to defend its claim to being a force for improving the world if it pulls out and leaves Iraq and its neighbors in turmoil. It is surely inconceivable — whatever the wild assertions of the 2008 presidential candidates about how many combat troops will stay in Iraq or go home—that the United States would exit in a manner that surrenders any influence it might still retain.

Indeed, the bitter benefit of Iraq—and America's best defense, years from now—may be that managing the fallout from the conflict has demanded the sustained engagement of the superpower in a region that, even if Saddam Hussein had stayed in power, was likely not going to stay peaceful and would have needed its attention.

Toppling the Dictator

The image of the statue of Saddam Hussein toppling into the square below, pulled down by jubilant Iraqis, is the one that America went to war to find. The memory is now hollow, given what followed.

All the same, it is worth keeping in mind that Saddam was exceptionally unpleasant, even in a harsh part of the world. He directed that brutality particularly against the Shias, some 60 percent of the population, and the Kurds in the north, 20 percent, killing men, women, and children—indeed, whole villages—who opposed him, sometimes with chemical weapons. That would have been stronger as a partial justification for war had the worst outrages been recent, rather than a decade earlier, but there was no shortage of evidence of Saddam's brutality up to the end.

What is more, his regime was working out how to evade the sanctions imposed after his 1990 invasion of Kuwait and his defeat by international forces. Russia, in particular, was keen to begin trading again with Iraq, and there are good reasons to think the sanctions regime would have crumbled within years. The lesson of that experience is not that such sanctions don't work — evidently, as we now know, they prevented him from getting the nuclear and chemical weapons he sought — but that they are very hard to keep in place over the years, as opportunistic countries wriggle to open links again with the pariah.

Saddam's outrages, and the threat of the weapons he might acquire, were not, on their own, anything like adequate justification for going to war, not in international law, nor in the politics of the United Nations Security Council, nor in the wider historic sense of "a just war."[1] But they were an important step on the road to making that case, had the rest of it been better.

It wasn't. The administration's intelligence on those threats was slim, as it turned out, and its presentation of that evidence duplicitous, as were its claims of links between Saddam Hussein and Al Qaeda. Its claim to have just cause for war crumbled when its forces failed to find weapons of mass destruction.

Of course, intelligence can always be wrong, but after the spectacle of its abuse by the Bush administration (and, for that matter, by the Blair government), voters, armed forces, and other nations are not going to accept again that they should take it on faith. And it is impossible to say without extraordinary blitheness that what replaced Saddam is better, given the death toll. Ordinary Iraqis have to live with more violence, and with local "mini-Saddams," even if the dictator is gone.

But it is still worth acknowledging that in the tangle of motives which took the Bush administration to war (not least, many have speculated, George W. Bush's desire to outdo his father), one of the guiding inspirations was a very American faith in democratic values and traditions—liberal values in the classic sense of the word. Reams have already been written about how the neoconservatives who so influenced the White House and Pentagon drew on that philosophy and turned it into a battle plan. It would be wrong to call Donald Rumsfeld and Vice President Dick Cheney anything other than old-fashioned conservatives, but Paul Wolfowitz, as Rumsfeld's deputy at the Pentagon, was one of the neocons best placed to influence them. Those advisers were grotesquely crude in applying their beliefs to Iraq without care for the circumstances of that country or for the costs of getting it wrong. Their dream of an American-friendly, democratic Middle East now looks farcical. In Iraq, the ideal was made hideous by its use to justify every decision, graced with flippant slogans, of which perhaps the worst was Donald Rumsfeld's "Freedom's untidy," on April 11, 2003, when he was irritated by questions about the looting of Baghdad. But it was a dream rooted in a profound faith in a philosophy which has at other times produced some of the best impulses of American policy.

That is one of several reasons why it is perverse to claim that the war was "all about oil," as many try to do (a brigade that was given unexpected support in September 2007 by Alan Greenspan, former chairman of the Federal Reserve, in his memoir). Saddam Hussein hardly deprived the world's oil markets of his country's production, nor could he, in any obvious way, have deprived America of it, given that Iraq's contribution simply adds to the total supply of a commodity.

It is striking that the idealism of the war's planners was shared by so many bright American officials in Iraq immediately after the invasion, even if tempered with a better appreciation of the obstacles. Many of them were very young, as accounts of the aftermath have noted, but some were not, and they brought their professional experience to bear on the predicament, together with a conviction in what they were doing. I remember one conversation in Baghdad in June 2003, three months after the invasion, when the worst problems appeared to be the sabotage of electricity pylons. An official from the General Accounting Office in Washington, sent in to try to bring order to the government departments, acknowledged freely how seductive Americans still found the images of the cheering crowds liberated by America in Paris more than sixty years ago, and how disconcerted Americans in Iraq had been not to encounter the same reaction. But that was not a confession of naïveté, exactly—more a wry acknowledgment of his country's mentality, combined still with a deep personal belief that Iraq could be improved. One of the most moving points of *No End in Sight,* the movie and later the book by Charles Ferguson, of the Council on Foreign Relations, is the chronicle of enormously bright Americans who threw their energies into trying to make the transition in Iraq work, and believed for some time that they could.

Democracy in Iraq

The failure so far of democracy to take proper root in Iraq is a blunt lesson to the United States in why such an enterprise demands much more than elections. For a democracy to work, minorities, or the losing side in elections, have to be able to go about their daily lives regardless of who is in power, and to have faith that in future elections they might win. Otherwise, they have every incentive to keep fighting.

To protect minorities or those not in power, there must be a constitution that sets out their rights. There must be courts which will uphold that fairly. There must be police to enforce it (and Kosovo and Northern Ireland show how long it can take to establish fair policing, trusted by all sides, in a deeply split community).

Iraq is not at that point, and it may not get there. The greatest obstacle to its embrace of democracy, and to peace, is the disinclination of the Shia majority, now in charge after years of brutal suppression by Saddam, to share any power with the Sunnis who were his elites. The 2007 "surge" of U.S. troops brought down the violence, but it did not cure the paralysis at the heart of government: the refusal, every time it came to the wire, of Shia leaders to share power and oil revenue with Sunnis or the Kurds in the north.

America was not wrong in believing that its own federalism held the key to the future structure of Iraq—in theory. That model still represents the ideal of how to weld together a country of very different groups. But America was unconsciously blithe about the difficulty of getting there in a country where the factions loathe one another. It forgot how long it took to put its own Constitution and Bill of Rights in place, and how rare the success of its own federation has been in assuming that Iraq would fall into the same model. It was also guilty of wanting it both ways — wanting to install democracy, but also wanting to pick the people who would emerge on top.

That does not mean that the pursuit of democracy should be avoided. But Iraq shows that it cannot be enforced. And if one side does not want to share power with the others, as is the case in Iraq now, it will take a long effort of intervention by outsiders, which may still fail, to persuade it that it should.

"Big Mistakes"

I am not going to attempt to defend America on its handling of the aftermath of the invasion, other than to say that there may have been almost no "right" way to do it, given the deep political obstacles to democracy I have just described. Every time a problem has been solved, by military commanders or by administrators, it has run back into that same lethal unwillingness of a Shia-led government to share power.

Given that, it becomes secondary to ask what might have been done differently.

The flippant answer is "everything," and America has no defense against the charge of astounding incompetence. In Iraq, America fought the war it wanted to fight, not the one that was there, determined that it should be like the liberation of Germany and France after the Second World War, its greatest triumph, and not like the counterinsurgency of Vietnam, its worst defeat.

The years since the invasion have seen a bitterly comical blame game as the protagonists write books to defend their own actions and fault others. It is now commonplace to say that three mistakes taken as fundamental caused Iraq to deteriorate so fast after the invasion. The first was the failure to stop the looting of Baghdad, and then, two decisions for which Paul Bremer, the American administrator, has been pilloried: the disbanding of the Iraqi army and the concurrent program of "de-Baathification" — stripping everyone senior in Saddam Hussein's party from a position of authority. Some critics would add to this list the failure to hand over sovereignty early to Iraqis; that is certainly what many Iraqis themselves say.[2]

The charge is fair. *Fiasco,* published in 2006 by Thomas Ricks, the *Washington Post*'s Pentagon reporter, is the best account of who said what in 2003 and 2004.

The book is a brilliant portrait of denial of the burgeoning trouble on the ground. Ricks is particularly astute on the clashes, not just the now-notorious one between the Pentagon and the State Department, but between the civilian and military sides of the Pentagon as well.

Nevertheless, decisions were never as simple as the retrospective accounts of "big mistakes" now portray. For example, the decision to disband the Iraqi army was premature and extraordinarily damaging, yet there is a case that, as it was, dominated by Sunnis, the army would not have held together under the ethnic strains that emerged. Senior officers in the coalition have made that point to me with some force. Much the same could be said of the de-Baathification — something had to be done to remove the Saddam supporters, although the policy went too far (as the attempts to reverse it in 2007 have acknowledged).

As Sir Hilary Synnott, Britain's first ambassador in Iraq, has argued, it is too easy to say that the mission was doomed.[3] But the scale, complexity, and speed of the problems which faced America once it toppled Saddam meant that it was almost impossible to pick the "right" path through them quickly enough to forestall the rise of ethnic violence. Barbara Bodine, a career Foreign Service officer and former ambassador to Yemen charged with overseeing the administration of Baghdad during the first few months of the occupation, has said that she believes that with the right planning, the occupation could have succeeded. But she viewed the obstacles this way: "There were 500 ways to do it wrong, and two or three ways to do it right. What we didn't understand is that we were going to go through all 500."[4]

Never Again?

Part of America's defense must be that it has quickly learned some of the lessons from Iraq, and that its own institutions have changed to make any repetition less likely. Its allies might forgive it for the mistakes of Iraq (although many Iraqis will not) if it can make that case. Congress has little power to determine the president's foreign policy, but all the same, its supine stance in the months before the Iraq invasion represents a failure of the system's checks and balances, which it now has every incentive to correct.

Congress's passivity was partly a reflection of the Republican majority in the Senate and House of Representatives, and the consequent inclination to support a Republican president. In 2002 and 2003, Congress failed to challenge either the intelligence about Saddam's weapons or the postwar planning. Criticisms did bubble up, mainly from Democrats, but won no purchase on the parade of administration officials before congressional committees. In the main hearing into the looming invasion held by the Senate Foreign Relations Committee, Senator Russell Feingold asked, "Why do we give the president a blank check to go ahead with this before we had the answers to these questions?" Few of his colleagues listened. Indeed, when push came to shove, many Democrats (including, notably, Hillary Clinton), fearful of looking soft or unpatriotic, voted to authorize the invasion.

The much more aggressive, questioning stance of the Senate Armed Services Committee since President Bush's 2004 reelection, as the American military toll in Iraq has been rising, suggests that it has learned a lesson, although that can be tested properly only by the passage of time. Some of that change came when the Democrats, who had no inclination to accommodate Bush, took control of the committee. But a good number of Republicans grew nervous about the war's impact on their own reelection prospects and also felt they had been misled by the Bush administration. That makes it likely that members of both parties will challenge the president more on future decisions to take military action.

One of the most striking signs that America is determined to learn the lessons of Iraq is in the U.S.

Army's new operations manual, the first since 2001, which officials began briefing to members of Congress early in 2008. This comprehensive doctrine of how the army thinks it should fight a war now elevates the goal of stabilizing nations after conflict to exactly the same level as winning in battle.

It is hard to overstate the change in attitude this represents. It has come after searing self-criticism by the army, which tries to draw lessons from failure perhaps more systematically than any other branch of American public life. (Among others, Colonel H. R. McMaster, the commander during a successful 2005 battle in northern Iraq, accused the army of "self-delusion" about the character of the conflict. In a paper for the International Institute for Strategic Studies, a London- and Washington-based think tank, he said that the army had placed an exaggerated faith in military technology and had neglected the skills of building the peace.) The army's new manual reflects the warning by Robert Gates, defense secretary, that counterinsurgency, Iraq-style, may be the future norm. If that is right, then the changes mean that America will not be as colossally unprepared as it was in Iraq, and much more able to tackle those new threats.

America will be judged not only by what has happened in Iraq, but by what is yet to happen, and by its willingness to try to repair the problems in Iraq and in the region. The military "surge" of 2007 was followed by a sharp drop in violence, down from hundreds of Iraqi deaths a day to dozens, but though a relief, the comparative calm is fragile in the absence of a political deal between Shias and other groups. Deciding whether America can still push them toward that deal through its presence in Iraq is one of the most difficult decisions Bush has left behind.

———

Chapter 8

THE INDEFENSIBLE: GUANTÁNAMO AND TORTURE

Any defense of America stops short of Guantánamo. The prison camp America set up at its naval base on the southeastern flank of Cuba is an offense to the values it says it is upholding in its "War on Terror." So are the practices, amounting to torture, that the Bush administration has deployed and which it continues to try to defend. The pity of it is that the United States should have found it easy to avoid the Guantánamo predicament.

Every time I write about Guantánamo in *The Times* I get a torrent of online comments from Americans saying that no one else has a right to comment. "You mind your business, we'll mind ours," was one of the more polite.[1] Expressed more subtly, that is the attitude of American diplomats abroad: irritation and bafflement that any other country should think it of concern what happens to no more than several hundred suspected terrorists collected from some of the world's least pleasant neighborhoods. They dispute that this one action of setting up the base, carried out in pursuit of the terrorists who planned the September 11 attacks, should lead to the forfeiting of international support, and they move quickly on to saying that they don't care if it does.

The Problem with Guantánamo

I was sitting at Guantánamo Bay one night in April 2006, after a week watching pretrial hearings, looking out at the Caribbean in the dark and thinking, "This is such a stupid mess for America to get itself into." In the heat of its response to September 11, the United States decided that it was justified in suspending its own principles of presuming someone innocent until proven guilty, of not holding someone without charge, of the right to a fair trial, of not using torture.

It's worthwhile to spell out what is wrong with Guantánamo because three-quarters of the e-mail I get on the subject from the United States professes absolutely no recognition that there is anything wrong with it. ("Thanks for treating our lives so lightly," said one typical comment in February 2008, the writer wrongly believing that I was arguing for the release of all those at Guantánamo.)

In the early days, when the world was transfixed by images of orange jumpsuits and goggles, and prisoners shackled to gurneys being moved between wire cages, the furor was about the harsh treatment of the captives. Although there are still serious legal challenges about maltreatment or torture, "Camp X-Ray," the site of those wire cages, is now abandoned; hummingbirds hover over the yellow flowering vines that have smothered the cells, and the interrogation room is a bare, sunny hut smelling of timber in the heat. The captives are now kept in purpose-built cells in "Camp Delta," two hundred feet from the edge of a cliff, although a double ring of green mesh blocks the sea view. Many are in solitary confinement, although the "most compliant" are free to congregate ("This block is a free-range camp," said the deadpan army captain showing me around).

The offense of Guantánamo boils down to two issues: the principle of holding people indefinitely without charge, and the new procedures of the military trials or "commissions" the United States has devised to try the very few captives whom it has charged, which do not give the accused the usual rights of conventional military or criminal courts. In spring 2008, there were 275 captives left in Guantánamo—less than half of the number that have passed through the camp. But the controversies do not dwindle as the numbers shrink, as they apply equally to other bases, such as the detention center at Bagram in Afghanistan, where in early 2008, the United States held 630 captives. At least Guantánamo has had a spotlight of international attention directed on it; the others have not.

Clinging to the Edge of Cuba

The United States claims the right to use the deep Cuban bay under a lease dating from 1903, which it held on to through the 1959 coup by Fidel Castro, although the former Cuban leader refuses to cash the annual $4,000 rent check. The struggles of an unbending military culture to resist the charm and untidiness of the Caribbean would be comical were it not for the grimness of the detention camp. For the eight thousand-odd military personnel crammed into what was, before 9/11, a sleepy naval base, there are sunset cruises, with guests segregated by rank of spouse, playgrounds with nothing to shield the metal climbing bars from scorching sun, and a lone McDonald's urging customers to "celebrate the month of the military child."

The sole purpose of putting a camp here—on the edge of an island with whose president America was not on speaking terms—was to claim that because the prison was not located in America, the United States did not have to apply American laws there. But the sight of the world's most powerful country in flight from its own jurisdiction has understandably provoked scorn, and legal challenge.

Holding People Without Charge

More than six years after Guantánamo received the first captives in January 2002, it is clear that the United States is in a position to bring cases against only a tiny minority of those it has detained. Indeed, by early 2008, the United States had charged only eighteen people at Guantánamo with offenses.[2] Pentagon officials venture that they hope eventually to charge about seventy of the total of more than six hundred who have passed through the prison.

Nevertheless, the United States still claims the right to hold the rest without charge. Its tortuous arguments for doing so have provoked sustained legal challenges. The American government argues that its captives are not traditional prisoners of war entitled to the protections of the 1949 Geneva Conventions, on the grounds that they are not soldiers of a recognized force, with identifiable uniforms. This makes them, the argument goes, "enemy combatants," and, when at Guantánamo, "detainees," a ludicrous verbal evasion of the straightforward label "prisoners."

One consequence of that evasion is that the Pentagon refused at first to confirm the names of those at the detention camp. Only on May 15, 2006, in response to an Associated Press Freedom of Information request and lawsuit, did it finally release a comprehensive list of all those who had been detained. Until then, lawyers and rights groups had tried to piece together a list from reports of those released, and by searching countries where the United States had collected captives, asking families if they thought that they might have a relative held in Cuba.

The first objection to the Guantánamo detentions is that the United States has not complied with the requirement of the Geneva Conventions to establish that the captives are indeed fighters and not unconnected bystanders, easily mistaken in the heat of conflict. The United States says that it has done so, through the "Combatant Status Review Tribunals," interview panels carried out in 2004 and 2005. But defense lawyers, including those appointed by the

Pentagon who are military officers in uniform themselves, have argued that these tribunals are entirely inadequate. Many of the captives from Pakistan and Afghanistan, according to their lawyers, were handed over to American forces by bounty hunters in return for about five thousand dollars. In the tribunals, they did not have access to a lawyer and were not able properly to contest the evidence against them.

The credibility of the tribunals is also undermined by the assertions, from President Bush downward, that all captives were guilty. From the beginning, President Bush called the Guantánamo occupants "killers," and Donald Rumsfeld, defense secretary, in January 2002, called them "among the most dangerous, best-trained, vicious killers on the face of the Earth."[3] Yet until September 2006, when the CIA transferred fourteen "high-value prisoners" to the base, it held no one of more significance than Salim Hamdan, a Yemeni who had been Osama bin Laden's driver.

A deeper objection to the detentions is that they offend the principle of habeas corpus, a historic principle usually described as deriving from the Magna Carta and a founding principle of U.S. law. Under that principle, the state is not entitled to hold someone without charging him. Guantánamo illustrates precisely the risk from which the founders wanted to protect people—that a government might detain people indefinitely, or preventively, for fear of crimes they had yet to commit. It sounds like a technical and antique protection, but the suspension of habeas corpus is considered one of the gravest actions an American president can attempt, on a par with suspending other fundamental freedoms such as freedom of the press and religion. It means that the president can say who might be a threat, and on his word alone, without evidence, have that person locked up.

The Military Commissions

The second flank on which the United States has opened itself to attack — again, unnecessarily — is in the use of specially devised "military commissions" to try the few whom it does charge. Administration officials argue that these new courts, with their new rules about evidence and procedure, are needed in the "War on Terror." They claim, for example, that the circumstances of seizing their captives do not allow them to gather evidence of enough rigor to stand up in a conventional court, and that in any case, because of heightened security, they might want to keep evidence secret and not show it to defendants — even though that means the defendants cannot challenge the claims. To that, the obvious retort is that if convictions cannot be secured without these special measures, they should not be secured at all. As a final sting in the process, the administration claims the right to continue holding the captives even if they are acquitted, because it defines them as "belligerents" in the "War on Terror" and will feel obliged to release them only when that war is over.

I spent a week at Guantánamo in April 2006 to see the pretrial hearings for the first ten captives to be charged, the first chance to hear the men speak since they had been captured, although no sensitive intelligence was introduced at that stage. The problem that the United States had created for itself was evident from the moment the proceedings began. It was a military environment down to the last detail: the judge, or "presiding officer," was a navy captain; the prosecutor was from the air force; the defense lawyer was from the army; all were in dress uniform. As a security precaution, even the metal spiral bindings had been removed from notebooks, just in case of an assault clearly impossible in such guarded circumstances.

Despite the appearance of extreme order, the proceedings were legal chaos. Two of the first three captives began by refusing to deal with their Pentagon-appointed lawyers, saying that they did not recognize the court's legitimacy. The lawyers then said that as they had, in effect, been fired, they had to respect their "clients'" wishes and desist from "defending an empty chair." The judge, as their senior military officer, ordered them to continue. The defense lawyers replied that they needed to ask the state bar associations to which they were affiliated whether they had to put their obligations as serving members of the armed forces above those as lawyers. As the state bar associations slowly started phoning back their varying answers, other lawyers leapt up from the two rows of audience to offer to defend the defense lawyers. The prisoners, in their first outing from the cells in four years, looked stunned.

Those stop-start uncertainties were just one symptom of the illness that plagued the new system — the need to make up its rules as it went along (almost always to the defendants' disadvantage, the defense lawyers said). The commissions also failed to meet basic standards of a fair trial, argued Colonel Dwight Sullivan, for years head of the team of Pentagon defense lawyers assigned to the defendants. Until late 2006, prisoners did not have the right to hear classified evidence against them (which might be simply the allegations of another prisoner at the base). Defendants' rights and ability in practice to challenge that evidence was inadequate, said Sullivan; their right to call witnesses was in doubt, and so was their right to pick lawyers to represent them. Most controversially, the evidence against them might have been obtained through torture, of them or others.

It is worth adding that the Pentagon-appointed defense lawyers don't claim their clients are necessarily innocent, or that any charges should be dropped—they simply want their clients to face a fair trial, as they would under existing court procedures. "We want the old rules," said Lieutenant Colonel Bryan Broyles, representing one of the prisoners. Colonel Morris Davis, the colorful chief prosecutor until 2007, once compared prosecuting the Guantánamo captives to "dragging Dracula into the sunlight."[4] But in early 2008, even he had become a critic of the process. Davis went so far as to offer to testify on behalf of at least one defendant, on the grounds that the commission had "a potential for rigged outcomes" and that he had "significant doubts about whether it would deliver full, fair, and open hearings."[5]

By spring 2008, only one trial had been completed—that of David Hicks, an Australian who pleaded guilty in March 2007 to charges of providing material support for terrorism, as part of a plea bargain after five years at Guantánamo. Under the deal, he returned home to serve a nine-month sentence and was set free in December 2007. This was not a help to the United States' claim to have collected the world's most dangerous terrorists.

Legal Challenges

The best that can be said in the United States' defense is that Congress and the Supreme Court have steadily challenged the administration's views on Guantánamo. Admittedly, that is a slender argument, and to someone waiting more than six years at Guantánamo, one that is grotesquely inadequate. But one of the things worth defending about America is the power of Congress and the courts to challenge the president's decisions as well as the explicit protections for the individual in the Bill of Rights. In a landmark ruling, the Supreme Court said in 2004 that the United States could not claim that Guantánamo was outside its control, and that prisoners there had the right to challenge their detention in U.S. courts. Two years later, in a complex and far-reaching case brought by a captive named Salim Hamdan, the Supreme Court ruled that enemy combatants were protected by the Geneva Conventions, that President Bush did not have the authority to create new tribunals without Congress's backing, and that conspiracy was not a war crime under the Uniform Code of Military Justice, the foundation of military law in the United States.[6]

To address the Court's point about the illegality of the tribunals, President Bush asked Congress to back new legislation to authorize the military commissions. It did so, and the 2006 Military Commissions Act amends some of the points that were most criticized, qualifying the Court's right to accept evidence obtained "under duress" and improving the defendant's right to hear all the evidence against him. But it leaves intact the president's right simply to define what constitutes torture and to say who is an "enemy combatant," and asserts the United States' right to hold such people without charging them and without limit—precisely the power the founders sought to restrict.

Lawyers acting on behalf of those detained at Guantánamo continue to challenge the administration's contention that habeas corpus does not apply to "enemy combatants." Two separate congressional bills in 2007 proposed the "restoration of habeas corpus." For now, though, the uncharged remain in their cells.

Torture

Guantánamo is interlinked with the issue which continues to do extravagant damage to the United States' reputation: its defense of the use of torture on suspected terrorists, or at least the use of techniques that to most people would be indistinguishable from torture. The United States has not actually come out and said that it embraces torture as a policy, in contravention of its own laws and international laws and treaties. But it has argued either that proposed techniques don't meet the definition or that the "War on Terror" allows exemptions.

This is an evasion of its own long tradition, stretching back to George Washington. In 1777, in an order covering prisoners taken in the Battle of Princeton, he wrote: "Treat them with humanity, and let them have no reason to Complain of our Copying the brutal example of the British Army in their treatment of our unfortunate brethren.... Provide everything necessary for them on the road."

Among the United States' main international commitments to the principle of not using torture (but by no means the only ones) are its ratification in 1955 of the four Geneva Conventions and its ratification in 1994 of the United Nations Convention against Torture (although it appended reservations about the scope of the definition of torture). It passed a federal statute in 1994 against torture and added the War Crimes Act of 1996, while its Uniform Code of Military Justice constrains what its armed forces can do in their treatment of captives.

But the Bush administration has employed an assortment of arguments that these layers of laws should not now constrain what it does in the "War on Terror." In 2002, in the now notorious "torture memos," the Department of Justice and the Pentagon drew up arguments limiting the definition of torture to the most extreme mistreatment that might lead to permanent injury or even death. Administration lawyers have also argued that because the "War on Terror" was a war, the president was a wartime commander in chief and so had the authority to set aside U.S. and international law. They also tried to maintain — until the Supreme Court disagreed in 2006 — that "enemy combatants" were not covered by the ban on torture in the Geneva Conventions.

This came to a head in September 2006, when the administration transferred fourteen "high-value prisoners" to Guantánamo from secret CIA "black prisons" in other countries, the first time it had acknowledged the existence of those sites. Among the transferred captives was Khalid Sheikh Mohammed, whom the United States accused of being the architect of the September 11 attacks and formally charged with killing the 2,996 victims.[7]

But the trials posed a problem because the CIA had used extremely harsh interrogation techniques with Mohammed. It acknowledged that he and two others had been "waterboarded"—a notorious practice which simulates the feeling of drowning.[8] Many, including some of President Bush's close allies, considered waterboarding to be torture.

The controversy erupted again in February 2008 when the Pentagon said it would seek the death penalty against six suspects it claimed were directly involved in the September 11 attacks. To try to preempt a legal challenge, the administration ordered a repeat of the CIA interviews by a "clean team" from the FBI. The new teams used time-tested bonding techniques, U.S. officials said, including giving the suspects Starbucks coffee.[9] But the revelation that the CIA had destroyed hours of tapes recording its interrogations opened the way to a further flood of legal challenges from Guantánamo defendants—exactly what the CIA had presumably wanted to forestall.

More generally, the White House stuck to its position that the United States should be allowed to use harsh treatment. On March 8, 2008, President Bush vetoed an intelligence bill which would have prevented the CIA from using waterboarding and other harsh interrogation techniques, and which would have limited the agency to the nineteen techniques in the army field manual. "I cannot sign into law a bill that would prevent me, and future presidents, from authorizing the CIA to…[take] all lawful actions necessary to protect Americans from attack," Bush said.[10]

However, even some of his former officials disagreed with him. Richard Armitage, the deputy secretary of state from 2001 to 2005, has argued openly, "Whether it's sleep deprivation or waterboarding, it is torture. It is a horrible blot on our national values and conscience."[11]

Where Should They Go?

American officials, particularly diplomats abroad, have developed a fluent line presenting Guantánamo as a practical problem, not an ethical dilemma. If there were only a home for these people, they declare, then America would shut the camp immediately. In London, the American ambassador and his deputy have devoted a good portion of their working hours to arguing this point. "Why don't you take them?" they have said to other governments.

In fact, Britain did just that, taking back nine British citizens in 2004 and 2005; it released them immediately, and some have gone on to become minor celebrities on what you might call the human-rights circuit. Britain also agreed to take back five more who had the status of legal residents but were not citizens.

But the United States has found it harder to get rid of others. In 2006, it persuaded Albania to take five Uighurs, a group of Muslims who feel persecuted within China. It still had seventeen left at Guantánamo, part of a group living in Afghanistan at the time of the invasion. Yet although the United States acknowledged that it was not going to try the men and did not regard them as a threat, it could not send them back to China for fear they would be persecuted there, and could not find other governments to take them for fear of offending Beijing.

This plaintive plea—presenting Guantánamo as a mere matter of resettling unwanted and now embarrassing dependents—sidesteps the issue of why the United States picked up the men in the first place, and its inadequate procedures for separating those it could plausibly suspect of terrorism from bystanders.

International Reaction

Britain has been the sharpest of the United States' close allies in criticizing Guantánamo, the procedures for trial, and the flirting with torture. Given Britain's stand in supporting America in Iraq and

Afghanistan, this criticism has been particularly high-profile and has become a point of difference between the two countries. "The historic tradition of the United States as a beacon of freedom, liberty and of justice deserves the removal of this symbol," said Lord Goldsmith, attorney general, on May 10, 2006.[12]

Since Tony Blair stepped down as prime minister, and since Britain began to pull out of Iraq, politicians have been even more sensitive to the political damage that association with Britain's closest and more controversial ally can bring. In early 2008, David Miliband, foreign secretary, had to apologize to Parliament that the United States had only just told Britain that the CIA had used the British overseas territory of Diego Garcia for two secret "rendition" flights of prisoners to Guantánamo and Morocco. His predecessor Jack Straw and Tony Blair had previously assured the House of Commons, based, they said, on assurances from Washington, that no such flights had taken place.

Other than Britain, European countries have been more muted in direct criticism of Guantánamo, although wanting to distance themselves from practices of rendition and torture. But they, too, have seized on the base as evidence of America's apparent inhumanity and indifference to legality in the pursuit of its "War on Terror."

Many Americans argue that their response to 9/11

is their business alone. As one *Times* online reader in Ohio put it: "Please tell me why I should give a damn about what the world thinks when 3000 AMERICANS (let me repeat: AMERICANS) died on 9/11. Had 3000 Euros died, then maybe you could have a say." [13]

The most trivial response to this sentiment is to note that a sixth of those who died on 9/11 were not American. Another point worth mentioning is that the United States is relying on other countries' help in the war in Afghanistan and generally, in pursuing terrorism. But the strongest argument is that if America shows no interest in international constraints on such behavior — even the laws and conventions it has drawn up itself — others need not either.

Britain and Terror Laws

That charge of treating such principles too lightly might be directed at Britain as well — and unlike America, it cannot argue that it has a Constitution that might correct the tendency. Although Britain has taken a stand of high principle on Guantánamo itself, the governments of Tony Blair and Gordon Brown have pursued a murkier approach to the protection of civil liberties in the pursuit of terrorism. In the Prevention of Terrorism Act 2005, the government brought in "control orders" which impose an unlimited range of restrictions on a person it suspects of terrorism, including bans on speaking to other named people, on leaving the house, and on where the person can go. As Liberty, a British civil liberties advocacy group, has argued, these rules "undermine the presumption of innocence — allowing ministers to punish someone without requiring them to prove that they have committed any crime." The government has also extended the period during which terrorism suspects can be locked up from fourteen days to twenty-eight days, the longest among Western democracies, and it may try for a further extension.

As Britain lacks a unified written Constitution, its protection for individual rights is drawn from historic laws and principles. Legal challenges and a few stubborn judges have upheld the principles in some cases, but the protections are fragile compared to those laid down in the U.S. Constitution. That remains America's best answer to the abuses of Guantánamo.

The "War on Terror" Does Not Demand Extreme Remedies

The common retort to everything I have argued here is that the "War on Terror" demands new measures — that faced with terrorists who are prepared to lose their lives, we cannot afford the luxury of civil liberties. Tony Blair has used this justification, and Gordon Brown, as well as George W. Bush. But the claim that current threats require novel measures is always made by democratic governments seeking a justification for spying on their citizens, for censorship, or for moving briskly against those they think might be their enemies without the irritating constraints of law. It was invoked during the Second World War, when America interned about 120,000 people of Japanese descent, nearly two-thirds of them American citizens.

Yet that is to set aside what makes Western democracies civilized and humane. As *The Economist* put it: "To eschew such tools is to fight terrorism with one hand tied behind your back. But that — with one hand tied behind their back — is precisely how democracies ought to fight terrorism."[14]

If the "War on Terror" were truly a war, it would have a definable end, as well as a definable enemy. It would then be easier — although still not trivial — to make a case for the temporary removal of some liberties. The West did not, by and large, define the Cold War as that kind of war, demanding special intrusions into civil liberties (the ugly spasm of McCarthyism and its residues being an exception). You might argue that this played some part in its "victory" in that contest, making Western countries more successful, and more attractive by comparison with the Soviet bloc.

Terrorism may make people in the United States — or Britain — feel personally vulnerable to attack in a way that the Cold War did not. But it takes an enormous distortion to portray it as being as much of a threat to the existence of Western democracies as was the hostility of the Soviet Union, let alone one that justifies suspending the principles the West says it is defending.

In America's case, the behavior of President Bush's successors will be the only test of whether Guantánamo was an aberration or whether it comes to represent the settled views of a majority of Americans. Fortunately, the increasingly robust challenges mounted by Congress and the courts are signs that the Guantánamo mistake will be corrected, and America will be able to reclaim a moral authority more in line with its traditions.

Chapter 9

BE CAREFUL WHAT YOU WISH FOR

Critics of America should consider carefully whether they really want what they have wished for: an America more restrained, "back in its box," deferential to other countries — or, even, less successful. They are deluding themselves if they think this would make them better off. Luckily (for them as well as for the United States), for all the threats the United States now faces, it is likely to keep its position as the world's superpower.

Of course, it would be easy for critics to get some of their wishes. Potential threats to American power are real. The credit crunch of late 2007 and 2008, the slump of the housing market — these jolts to American economic success have followed straight on the shock of Iraq and its illustration of the limits that roadside bombs and AK-47s can place on the world's most powerful military machine. Russia, under President Vladimir Putin, has been sourly aggressive and may continue that way under his successor, Dmitry Medvedev. China is grabbing superlatives for itself — the fastest-growing economy, perhaps the largest soon[1] — even if it is also picking up unwanted titles, such as the largest polluter. Iran has not given an inch under American pressure to drop its nuclear ambitions and is steadily filling the power vacuum left in Iraq; the Arab world is scornful of the American project to export democracy; and the United States' neighbors to the south, led by Venezuela's Hugo Chávez, have mounted a noisy opposition to American-style capitalism.

Of these, the threats from Russia and China are the greatest, although they are usually exaggerated. Russia's behavior has been unpleasant, but its dreams of regaining its former power are a delusion; its oil and gas supplies are shrinking fast, and so is its population. China's growth is running into the predictable problems of lethal pollution and the stubborn independence of the provinces. Neither is a real military threat, even if China has the world's biggest army, at 2.1 million people, almost double that of America. It spends less than a tenth of America's military budget (estimates are tricky) — although it has raised its budget by half in just two years. Russia spends even less, although it is also diverting some of its new oil wealth to defense.

Iran is menacing, but it lacks support among Arab countries to be the force in the region that it wants. None of these countries is in a position to challenge American dominance. It is safe to talk about American preeminence for another generation; it is ludicrous to reckon that the twenty-first century might not be a second American Century, even if its position were less emphatically secure.

America's best response to those challenges is to promote its own values and rules, bringing as many countries as it can onto its side. Its powerful attractions, of openness and freedom, are its best response to the Arab world's disdain, or to Chávez's antagonism. It can best cope with Russia and China by drawing them into the international system of rules and institutions—and upholding them itself. That is working with China, which knows that its best economic hopes lie in trading with the rest of the world, and that the restrictions this will place on it are worth it. This approach has worked less well with Russia, but it has not entirely failed; Putin could have caused far more trouble than he chose to.

People in other democratic countries will be enormously better off if America retains its position as the world's superpower. To delight in its difficulties is to brush away their dependence on its prosperity and security.

It is easy to forget, outside America, the preoccupations the United States will face in the next few decades. Huge population growth, immigration, need for energy — those are plenty of reasons to incline it to turn inward and concentrate on its own problems and opportunities, not those of other countries, as in the past it regularly has.

An Inconvenient Truth

The world's close economic relationship with America is inescapable. The slide of 2007 and 2008 has been a reminder of that, as the American building boom stalled, and Americans had to grapple with falling house prices, higher oil and gasoline costs, and the drying up of credit. It is ridiculous to maintain that the rest of the world can be completely independent, although some try. In the spring of 2008, a representative of an Arab oil government walked into my office as the growing American financial crisis had just consumed Bear Stearns, looked at the television screen as reports of the renowned investment bank's fate filtered in, and said, "That's what I like to see, miserable Americans."

True, the slump in world markets in early 2008 prompted much talk about "decoupling"—the question of whether other countries can prosper even when the American engine is stalling. More than in the past is the answer—but no country is immune. Many hoped that the giants of the developing world—China, India, Russia, and Brazil—would be stable pillars, whatever happened in the United States. Even though their exports are now worth nearly half of their gross domestic product (doubling in less than two decades), most of that trade was with one another, or near neighbors, not the United States. In none of them does trade with the United States amount to more than 8 percent of their economies. Yet even in China, there was blunt acknowledgment of the damage an American recession could do. Zhang Tao, deputy head of the international department of the People's Bank of China, told a financial seminar in January 2008, "If US consumption really comes down, that's bad news for us. That will have a pretty severe impact on our exports."[2] Wang Jian, head of the China Society of Macroeconomics, agreed that China's growing trade with Europe was unlikely to insulate it from a drop in exports to the United States, because if Europe exported less to America, it would buy less from China. "Global demand is ultimately driven by the United States," he said.[3]

Smaller Asian countries are even more dependent on the United States; Singapore and Malaysia each send it exports worth more than a fifth of their economies. They are generally in better financial shape than in the 1997–1998 Asian crisis, but a prolonged American slump will still hit them. Shaukat Aziz, the former Pakistani prime minister, said in early 2008, "For us, decoupling is a myth. America suffers, we suffer."[4]

Nor is Japan a refuge. Since 2002, it has been climbing out of a long slump, pulled along by exporting to other countries. Its sales to China and Europe outstrip those to America, but it knows that many of its products that go to China as components end up in America as finished goods. Europe is in the same trap, even though the United States accounts for just 14 percent of the exports of the eurozone (the region that uses the euro currency, which includes most of the big European countries but not Britain). Those countries hope that by looking east, not west, they can find new markets, but if those too are affected by an American slowdown, they will find no escape there.

The cascading effects depend on the scale of the problems in America, but there is no point pretending that any country can entirely avoid them—or that it should be grateful for them.

Russia: Belligerent and Delusional

If there is a single reason why Europe cannot want America to be less engaged in international problems, it is Russia. The threat can easily be exaggerated — as it is by Russia itself, which insists on pretending that it is still a world power. It is not; it is the shell of a former empire, with nuclear weapons, and oil and gas, but an aging population of just 145 million, falling by more than half a million a year from alcoholism, drugs, and disease. Men's life expectancy is now just fifty-eight years, considerably lower than under the Soviet Union.[5]

All the same, its sour aggression does need countering, and the United States will play the prime part in doing that. Europe is too close, too ambivalent, and too nervous of Moscow's reaction (such as turning off the gas pipelines running westward, as it has shown it can) to do that well.

Hopes that the fall of the Soviet Union would lead to the emergence of a democratic and liberal Russia are now long gone. President Putin drew for justification of his authoritarian approach on the chaos of Boris Yeltsin's presidency and ordinary Russians' incredulous fury at the oligarchs, who became within a few years some of the richest people on the planet. But he also drew on the hurt pride after the collapse of the Soviet Union and the belief that surely it was just a matter of time before Russia reclaimed its empire. It is a fantasy, but one that seems to have sustained Putin as he chose to step up the aggressive rhetoric against the United States in the final year of his presidency. At a dinner at his residence outside Moscow in June 2007, he used America's plans to site missile defense bases in Poland and the Czech Republic as provocation for announcing that he might point Russia's nuclear missiles at Europe again for the first time since the end of the Cold War.[6]

Even more striking than this declaration, which, as presumably intended, grabbed the world's headlines for the week before the G8 summit of the biggest industrial countries, was his deep suspicion of America, which threaded through everything he said. Putin cited the latest Amnesty International report repeatedly through the four-hour dinner, finding in it an endless vein of abuses of human rights in the United States (and ignoring its lengthy criticism of Russia). Shortly afterward, he announced that Russia would suspend the Conventional Armed Forces in Europe treaty, which regulated how close to the border Russia and Europe would keep their armed forces.[7]

Oil at more than $100 a barrel has fed Russia's

dream of being able to act like a superpower, albeit one temporarily shrunken. An astute eye on Europe's need for energy, and care in signing deals on new pipelines have given Russia more leverage. But it can't last. Not only has Russia's wider economy not developed, but it has not invested much of this bonanza back into its oil industry, which remains wasteful and, in places, simply primitive.

Nor is Russia tolerant of foreign investment. In the oil industry, where the Kremlin has only briefly accepted foreign companies, it is busy rewriting their contracts to turn these firms into the equivalent of hired help—a sure way to prevent the technology transfer that can benefit both sides. That was the fate Royal Dutch Shell suffered in 2006 when Russia revoked, on "environmental grounds," its license for the $20 billion Sakhalin-2 oil and gas field, forcing it to sell a controlling stake. BP, the British energy company, has little to protect it if, as seems likely, Russia decides that its previous agreements were too generous given today's oil prices.

This rising tension comes at a point of particularly icy relations with Britain, because of a macabre episode in which the violent world of Russian agents and émigrés burst into the open in London's Piccadilly. In November 2006, Alexander Litvinenko, a former Soviet-era security agent, was murdered by polonium poisoning, apparently from lunch in a sushi bar. The radioactive substance (hard to obtain except from Russian government laboratories) had apparently been placed in his food. Litvinenko, who became a British citizen shortly before his death, used the time it took him to die in hospital to condemn the Kremlin, accusing President Putin of his murder. Russia has since refused to respond to Britain's extradition request for the man it believes carried out the killing.

Do these kinds of actions put Russia outside international laws and treaties? On the edge of them, certainly. A country that will not recognize commercial contracts is just a whisker away from defying all kinds of international law, trading resolutions, arms treaties, and so on. So is any country that murders another's citizens, let alone by James Bond–like methods.

Yet it would be an exaggeration to say that Russia has become a rogue state. The hope, in the eyes of Western diplomats, is that it is still picking fights one by one, on their merits, not for the mere sake of obstructing the West. The United States, Britain, and France have persuaded Russia to join them in the United Nations Security Council in putting sanctions on Iran for refusing to drop its nuclear ambitions. Nor has Russia caused as much mischief as it might have done when the Serbian province of Kosovo declared itself to be an independent country early in 2008, even though, as an old ally of Serbia, it could easily have encouraged violent uprising. It certainly agrees with the United States and Britain about the threat of Islamic fundamentalism, even if that leads to horrors like its treatment of Chechnya (about which Europe has been shockingly silent).

The best hope is to continue to give Russia incentive to work in line with Western interests, and the United States is better placed than Europe to do that, as the greater military power and also as an unchallengeable example of economic success.

China: Persuading It to Work Within Rules

There are so many forecasts of a coming clash between China and the United States that they almost count as a new kind of product, produced in bulk by both countries. Both want energy, and security, and trade on their own terms. Even though China has traditionally said the minimum about foreign policy, preferring to express itself through contracts signed, it has been openly contemptuous of democracy. In Kenya in January 2008, when protests at a rigged election killed hundreds, an editorial in the Communist Party's *People's Daily* declared that "Western-style democratic theory simply isn't suited to African conditions, but rather carries with it the root of disaster." China's leaders have argued that India is handicapped by its democracy from reaching Chinese rates of growth.

It is impossible to exaggerate the drama of the transformation China is conducting on itself. Lawrence Summers, the former U.S. treasury secretary, has pointed out that living standards in China will "rise 100-fold within a single human life span—more than living standards have increased in the United States since my country gained independence in 1776." He added, in a speech in Beijing in January 2007, that "what happens in Asia, the changes in the lives of so many people, so quickly, and its ramifications for the global system will be the most important story when the history of our times is written."[8]

So far, China is managing to secure itself supplies of energy and resources. It has been steaming through Africa, signing deals with governments (and imposing none of the conditions about democracy and good government that high-minded development agencies such as Britain's Department for International Development tend to attach). Its state-owned oil companies are competing hard to be among the first into Iraq, less perturbed than their Western counterparts by fears of violence or uncertain title to the resources.

But the question is whether that can continue. China's imports of oil will need to triple by 2030, according to the International Energy Agency. Pollution is beginning to brake its growth. According to the government's own estimates, the costs of that pollution in damaged health, undrinkable water, and lost agriculture could be a tenth of the gross domestic product.[9] China's new affluence also gives the provinces and even small communities the power to challenge Beijing, as Chinese leaders are well aware. Each year, there are tens of thousands of local protests, against everything from pollution to compulsory relocation orders. That doesn't mean China will become more democratic as it gets richer — just that as it gets richer, its leaders will find it harder to keep control. In an *Economist* magazine debate held in London's Chatham House in March 2006 under the title "India Will Overtake China in the Next 25 Years," almost all the panel and audience disagreed with the proposition but also felt that China was more capable of sudden turmoil and instability, and that its success was more vulnerable to fracture.

There are signs that China is beginning to realize that its interests lie in being closely connected to other governments and in following international rules. It joined the World Trade Organization in December 2001 after a fifteen-year battle and has begun to acknowledge that this is going to mean tightening up piracy of DVDs and not selling poisonous toys abroad.

The United States is well-placed to encourage this.

As John Ikenberry, professor of politics and international affairs at Princeton University, argued in a *Foreign Affairs* article in early 2008, "China…faces a Western-centered system that is open, integrated, and rule-based, with wide and deep political foundations…itself the product of farsighted US leadership." He added: "As it faces an ascendant China, the United States should remember that its leadership of the Western order allows it to shape the environment in which China will make critical strategic choices. If it wants to preserve this leadership, Washington must work to strengthen the rules and institutions that underpin that order — making it even easier to join and harder to overturn."[10]

China appears at least partly convinced of this case. It has agreed to back sanctions against Iran in the United Nations Security Council, even though the United States and Britain feared it would not support action against its trading partner and oil supplier. It has (if grudgingly) agreed to work with other countries to put pressure on North Korea over its nuclear program. And it was clearly shocked by Hollywood's protest against the genocide in Sudan's Darfur region ahead of the 2008 Beijing Olympics, culminating in Steven Spielberg's decision to withdraw as artistic director of the games. In a very rare move, it began putting pressure on Sudan, as its largest trading partner and international protector, leaning on it to accept an international peacekeeping force, sending engineers to help the force, and appointing a special envoy to the region. America will play a vital part in persuading China generally to take up this kind of role.

Iran: A Nuclear Bomb Within the Next Presidency?

The United States may find the same task harder with Iran, which is not giving way in its determination to hold on to its nuclear program. A now notorious American "National Intelligence Estimate," published at the end of 2007, punctured the United States' threats that it would not rule out military strikes if Iran did not back down. The report, by saying that it believed Iran had stopped designing the warheads of nuclear weapons, allowed Iran gleefully to claim the moral high ground — even though the report made clear that such work had taken place and that other potential preparations for a weapon were continuing.

But while the notion of attacking Iran regularly pulses through Washington, it has always been deeply unattractive — far worse than an invasion of Iraq. An invasion of Iran is unthinkable — it is a much bigger country, with about 65 million people compared to

Iraq's 27 million or so.[11] It has been helped by five years of high oil prices; it has an army of more than half a million, with 350,000 reservists as well.[12] You do not have to have many conversations in Tehran pizza parlors, their walls covered with photographs of ayatollahs but their menus all-American, to work out that an attack would make instant enemies out of the many Iranians who love the United States—the best hope for prizing the ayatollahs out of power. One Iranian told *Newsweek:* "As a gay man living in Iran"—a phenomenon that President Mahmoud Ahmadinejad has said doesn't exist—"I couldn't express myself and be what I am. My brother went to jail for eight years because he opposed this regime....Despite all that, if one day America or Israel attack Iran, I'll go back and defend my country."[13] A deliberate insult to Ahmadinejad from the president of Columbia University provoked an outpouring of support for him from ordinary Iranians, outraged at the snub to their country (which Ahmadinejad's blog gleefully recorded).[14]

Even an airstrike on Iran's nuclear targets would be formidably hard for the United States. Beyond the half-dozen known sites, Iran could have many hidden ones—and hundreds of missile silos as well. If America attempted a strike, the only likely member of the "coalition of the willing" would be Israel, though Iran's worried Arab neighbors might quietly be supportive. Many speculate that Israel might do the job on its own, but one Israeli officer explained to me in late 2007 why that seemed unattractive. "We'd get the retaliation [from Iran] either way, but the U.S. would do it better—they'd have the scale to hit more of the targets. So only if we were completely convinced the U.S. would never move, and that the threat had reached the point of warranting immediate action, would we consider that step."[15]

For all these reasons, the Bush administration has rightly been putting its efforts behind diplomacy, together with Europe. Seyed Mohammad Hossein Adeli, a former Iranian ambassador to London, said with a grin on leaving the post in November 2005, "My job was to drive a wedge between the U.S. and Europe."[16] British diplomats disagree that he achieved this goal, but there is no faulting the tactics. There are some signs now that the American drive to clamp down on Iranian banks is having an effect, which previous sanctions have not.

America Preoccupied at Home

The amount of effort Americans will want to put into these problems abroad will depend also on their stamina for handling change at home. The 2008 election campaign was an illustration — although easily overlooked outside America — of the difficult questions its politicians and people have to cope with in the immediate future. The population, which has just passed 300 million, is set to rise to 420 million by 2050. About half of that is projected to come from immigration and from immigrants' children, but half is the result of Americans' living longer.

That is an extraordinary wave of change for a country to handle, even before considering that many of the new people will be Hispanic. It begins to change the character of the country, pushing out the suburbs, stretching out the West and Southwest. It is a huge opportunity as well as a strain. It will leave America as the only big developed country with more children than pensioners, and with a growing population of working age.

But if you add to the issues on Americans' minds the problem of securing energy resources and of trying to wean parts of its economy off the use of large cars, it is clear that politicians have a hugely demanding task adjudicating between all these groups at home. For other countries, it will become harder to persuade Americans that they should continue to look outward to other problems, and should risk tens of billions of dollars and their soldiers' lives in doing so. As Michael Lind, of the New America Foundation in Washington, DC, argues, "The US is not going to be eclipsed any time soon by another superpower, but it may exhaust itself by allowing its commitments to exceed the resources that the public is willing to allot to foreign policy."[17]

The Superpower Is Not Facing Eclipse

Lind is surely right that it is much too pessimistic to predict the eclipse of the American superpower. On the contrary, Russia is in no position to challenge it, and China has enormous problems to overcome before it can realistically do so. But China's evolution, if it took a malign form, could still cause America and other liberal democracies great discomfort. So could Russia, if causing that discomfort came to seem, to its leaders, like the only attractive mission left to them.

The best way for the United States to manage those challenges is to persuade both countries to work within the system of rules and institutions it has helped build. For that, it needs other countries' help, particularly in Europe, but those countries in turn should not take America's effort for granted.

Chapter 10

HOW AMERICA COULD
HELP ITSELF

My mother, an American, was always amused after coming to live in Britain by the euphemism of "helping police with inquiries" for those who had just been arrested. "What helpful suggestions could you make?" she would say. "'Have you thought of looking in the river?'"

It seems just as presumptuous to advise a superpower on how to repair its world image and restore its influence abroad when it doesn't recognize the conversation. Bush administration officials, and many U.S. citizens, have often made it clear that they don't give a damn what others think. "Oh, the envy," said one comment from San Francisco on *The Times* Web site, about a piece criticizing the United States' refusal to sign a United Nations accord against an "arms race in space," where 160 countries voted in favor. "Most of the 160 get to work on a donkey,"[1] added the writer—and he was not the only one to express such sentiments.

All the same, I have offered here suggestions for change which would improve the predicament in which America finds itself after Iraq and President George W. Bush, as it faces a breathtaking range of challenges, with economic turmoil and worries about climate change adding to the list of ugly problems left around Iraq, Iran, and the Middle East. There are practical steps it could take to improve relations with countries that should be its allies and people who should be its natural supporters.

It should immediately drop policies, such as the detention camp at Guantánamo Bay, that it cannot justify by its own values. It should go a long way in softening its tone on those, such as climate change, where it has some justification for going its own way, but which are found so provocative by the rest of the world that they carry huge political cost. It should wean itself off those which represent a view of the world that it finds tempting—the "War on Terror," the threat of China—but which represent a paranoid exaggeration of the threat it faces and blind it to a better-judged response.

The changes would help retrieve the United States' authority in advocating its democratic values and its belief in a world governed by the rule of law and international treaties, which many people and governments are now challenging or rejecting altogether. The list may also be a balm for the self-laceration with which some Americans have tormented themselves during Iraq and the Bush years. There is a line beyond which the United States should not go in accommodating a planet full of critics. There are some actions for which it should apologize, but there is a limit—which comes early, I have argued—beyond which it should concede nothing. It should not apologize for its central values or for its essential difference from those who dislike its choices.

Elect a New President

The Economist commented toward the end of George W. Bush's presidency that "if America were a stock, it would be a 'buy': an undervalued market leader, in need of new management." It added: "But that points to its last great strength. More than any rival, America corrects itself."[2] America's unsurpassed tool for "correcting itself" is the election of a new president and Congress. The headiness felt in Britain, Germany, France—and of course in the United States itself—at the 2008 election campaign showed the exhilaration so many felt about the prospect of a new president, one who might allow Americans to feel good about their country again, and their allies not ashamed of their allegiance.

Give a Nod to Cooperation

The Bush administration, in its closing months, tried to make some correction itself, and became a partial convert to the notion of civility. It called together the Annapolis summit on the Middle East in November 2007, and tried hard not to wreck the international talks on climate change in Bali shortly afterward. It began working energetically within the United Nations system it had derided ahead of the Iraq invasion to secure tighter sanctions on Iran and a joint approach on Darfur. In November 2007, President Bush welcomed Nicolas Sarkozy, France's new president, as a good new friend. But fully repairing the Bush administration's relations with the world was a lost cause by mid-2007.

A mere change of tone from the abrasion of the Bush administration will not solve America's problems abroad, but it would be a start. It is not going to dissolve entrenched opposition within a United Nations whose instincts are often profoundly anti-American, nor is it going to erase the differences that run deep between America and Europe over the Middle East and the "War on Terror." But it would be a first defense against the charge that America is indifferent to the principle of a world governed by laws, unless they suit its own interests.

Act on Global Warming, the Economy, and Trade

A more substantial defense would be to pursue a serious deal with other countries on curbing climate change, one of the fastest ways for a new administration to say that it has brought change from the Bush years. Global warming is a problem too serious for America not to respond. Indeed, the prospect of severe upheaval to people's lives within the next fifty years outstrips the terrorist threat on which the Bush administration has put such weight, even if it is impossible to put good numbers on either probability. And climate change has taken on too much political resonance, in Europe and in the developing world, for America not to suffer badly from seeming like the world's villain.

The United States can justifiably argue that in the 1970s and 1980s, it helped bring environmental issues to the world's attention and — up to a point — that in its resistance to binding targets it is protecting the well-being its economic growth brings to itself and others. But it needs to show more willingness. American leaders have claimed that the United States can battle global warming by developing new technology; it needs to show that this is happening, and that such technology is being sold to the dirtier parts of the developing world. Luckily, the rise in the price of oil has done a lot of the work in kick-starting the search for energy efficiency.

An economic slump will make climate change targets easier to meet, although it may take some political momentum out of the movement as well, as attention switches to the turmoil in the financial markets and the threat of a crash in house prices. That economic challenge may be, for Bush's successors, as big as 9/11 was for him; it lacks the hideous drama, but it affects far more people, in America and abroad. Here other countries will look to America for leadership. That may not mean dramatic action — in such a crisis, there are always calls for ambitious new rules or institutions to prevent it happening again. But America could help by overhauling its antique and tangled regulation of banks, and by making careful decisions about when, if ever, to use taxpayers' money to bail out banks and people who can't pay their mortgages.

Unfortunately, trade talks are rarely made easier in tough times for the economy. Protectionism will rise, as countries fear that their own people's jobs will be lost. It would be a huge pity if the United States indulged itself in one of its spasms of protectionism when it is better placed than any other country to give the lead in promoting liberal trade. In particular, it would help to let go of its grotesque subsidies of nearly $20 billion a year paid to its dwindling band of farmers, which have outstripped even the European Union's notorious excesses in that realm.

Stop Demonizing China

Trade is America's best chance to pull China further within the laws and institutions of the developed world. It would help to tone down the fearmongering about China, an area where Congress presents a more extreme face to the world than do America's presidents (although European governments are now rivaling it). But the saber rattling and antagonism help America in nothing: not in enforcing trade rules, nor in racing to buy up energy supplies, nor in heading off the threat of nuclear proliferation in Iran, North Korea, and the Middle East.

That is not to say that China is benign. But America would get further by pointing out to China that engagement in these problems is in its own interest, and that its traditional distaste for involving itself in diplomacy is unsustainable.

Stay Engaged in Iraq and the Region

Economic threats may rival Iraq and the Middle East as the greatest challenge for President Bush's successor, but America will still be judged across the world by its handling of the Iraq debacle after Bush. It can pull out troops, but it cannot cut and run from the problem overall, out of responsibility to Iraqis and out of its own self-interest.

Part of that solution will be continuing to work to unblock the Israeli-Palestinian deadlock, to which the Bush administration gave only sporadic attention. The problem has worsened during that neglect, with the rise to power of the Hamas Islamist group and Israel's expansion of settlements on the West Bank, toward which Bush was extraordinarily accepting, even given that support for Israel is an unwavering commitment of American policy, no matter who the president. "Engagement" is an overused word, but it means, at the least, recognition that the United States is the only party that can put pressure on Israel to make the concessions that will be a central part of any deal. It also means persistence, even when a deal seems impossible, as now. It is an honorable principle that few situations are so bleak they cannot be improved, even if they cannot be resolved.

But for all the inflammatory power the conflict retains, in the images now instantly broadcast across the Arab world on Arabic television, it has arguably been eclipsed as a problem by the other consequences of the Iraq invasion — and the rise of Iran as a regional giant is the worst.

Consider Talking to Iran

Iran's determination to give itself the ability to make its own nuclear weapons — which it might manage during the American presidency after Bush's — is one of America's most difficult foreign problems. Bombing Iran's suspected nuclear sites — and there might be hundreds — was never attractive. But the unfortunately phrased conclusions of the National Intelligence Estimate, published at the end of 2007, allowed Iran to claim the high ground. The report asserted that Iran had stopped actually trying to design a nuclear warhead but did not give enough emphasis to its other conclusion that more difficult work, also crucial to making a weapon, had continued.

No option is attractive, but one clearly open to

Bush's successor—which Bush emphatically ruled out—is to consider talking to Iran about mutual interests for security in the region. The policy of withholding mere contact with the United States as punishment, a core tactic of the Bush administration, has manifestly not worked.

Work with Europe on Handling Russia

Iran would not be such a problem if it did not have Russia's support. It is overdramatic to pronounce the start of a new cold war, but Putin's threat in June 2007 to point nuclear missiles at Europe again, and his decision in December 2007 to send Iran the fuel for its first nuclear reactor, show he intends to defy the West where it has most explicitly asked for his help. For Britain and America, Putin's antagonism suddenly seemed to be coloring every issue: Kosovo, gas supplies to Europe, America's desire to base a new missile shield in Poland and the Czech Republic, and Russia's decision to suspend the Conventional Armed Forces in Europe treaty.

In all of these instances, Europe's interests are very close to those of America. But for the sake of getting on with Russia, and not provoking their huge neighbor, some countries have conceded it points that

America rightly does not want to do. At the NATO summit in April 2008, Germany blocked the United States' call to bring Ukraine and Georgia into the alliance, for fear of upsetting Russia. The United States took an honorable position in that argument—even if it knew it would lose—but to win those debates with Europe is going to take effort. America cannot take the alliance with Europe for granted, even if that means a degree of perpetual courtship which it feels should be unnecessary given the military protection it extends to the continent.

Don't Neglect Eastern Europe

On that note, America is in serious danger of neglecting the countries of Central and Eastern Europe, and of taking for granted their enthusiasm for all things American. Their expressions of gratitude to the United States when the Iron Curtain fell were genuine and overwhelming, but such loyalty is no longer automatic.

The Polish government elected in October 2007 promptly said that it would take its nine hundred troops out of Iraq by the end of 2008, and that the United States should not assume Poland would agree to host its missile shield. True, Poland's expectations of the new "special relationship" with Washington were too high. Some Polish commentators giddily talked of Poland's becoming a "second Israel" or a "United States supertanker on the waters of Eastern Europe." But Poland is just the loudest voice among countries which suddenly think they should hedge their bets in backing the superpower.

. . . Or Turkey

Much the same can be said for Turkey, where many feel aggrieved that the United States takes their country for granted despite its extraordinary value as a secular, democratic Muslim country, a supporter of Israel, the only Muslim member of the North Atlantic Treaty Organization, and host to American military bases. Parliamentarians voted in 2003 to refuse to allow the United States to use Turkish territory to open a northern front against Iraq. Although the United States made a last-minute offer of $6 billion in grants or $20 billion in loans, it was not enough to outweigh huge public opposition. But European diplomats in Ankara believed that the support would have been there had the United States spent more time in courting it.

Pick Friends Among Dictators
with More Care

While America has neglected valuable allies, it has too generously embraced unpleasant friends. To single out one country as a problem is to repeat America's own often ridiculous preoccupation with rogue states or leaders. But the United States' support for Pakistan's Pervez Musharraf is an unjustifiable compromise of its commitment to democracy. It is also shortsighted; it ignores the way Pakistan's military has awarded itself land and lucrative privileges, and become a cause of friction between social groups rather than the solution. Even judged just by the promotion of American interests, the support of such regimes won't work, given their inability, in the end, to contain their people's rising frustration.

Drop the Phrase "War on Terror" and
Close Guantánamo

Giving up the language of war may be hard for any American president to do; anything that sounds like faltering in the face of the United States' enemies will carry a political price. But keeping it carries a cost, too.

It alienates those in Europe who tend to find the term "War on Terror" an unhelpful conflation of different local threats, and who believe it invests terrorists with heroic grandeur when they should be regarded as criminals.

"The concept of war, which could be discounted in the early months after September 11 as a matter of semantics, is itself a polarizing factor in transatlantic relations," argues Gary Samore, director of studies at the Council on Foreign Relations in New York, together with colleagues at the International Institute for Strategic Studies think tank in London. Samore and his colleagues point out that European countries, with much larger Muslim populations than the United States, are not going to declare themselves at war in a way that offends a large proportion of their own people. Even given the shock to America of September 11, its "overwhelming preoccupation with terrorism that is implied by mobilization for war seems out of proportion to Europeans and many others. Terrorism is nowhere near the top of the list of concerns for most of the world."[3]

Preoccupation with the "War on Terror" has also led the United States into the entirely unnecessary mess of Guantánamo Bay, compromising its own claim to be defending principles of freedom and justice, and being condemned around the world for the sake of a few hundred captives, most of whom it does not have evidence to charge. It should try the captives in its own conventional courts or let them go and shut the camp—surely an irresistibly easy gesture for Bush's successor to make.

On that note, America should start dealing with Cuba, unwilling host to the Guantánamo camp. To see the world's superpower squatting on the edge of an island to evade its own laws is too much for the world to overlook. To see America waiting for one man and his brother to die before it agrees to talk to the island's government takes its behavior from the offensive to the ludicrous.

Take Care That the Visa Regime
Does Not Shut Out the Best

On a final note, the United States should take care that the new visa regime prompted by fears of terrorism does not shut out the best. The price the United States pays for rising anti-Americanism may include a subtle component: the students, businesspeople, and visitors who decide, perhaps nudged by the slightest margin of emotion, to throw in their lot with a different country. Their loss will be undetectable in the throngs of people still desperate to go to America, but that does not mean that it will not be real—a drop in the attraction of the most powerful magnet in the world.

The United States, complacent about the strength of its appeal, and righteously fearful about the threat it feels it faces from foreign terrorists, is in danger of repelling or shutting out some of the best and the brightest.

A Warning to Europe

Any successor of George W. Bush will want to seem different. Almost any will sound, in tone at least, keener on working with other countries. But Europe is going to be disappointed if it expects all the things it has disliked about Bush to fall away at the same time. That won't happen — and it shouldn't.

For a start, the Bush years have left Americans passionately divided about foreign policy in a way which will complicate the decisions it makes and the message the United States sends to the world. Those in other countries often fail to understand the impact of conflict in American politics, trying to read its policy entirely from the president and ignoring Congress. They may be expecting a simpler face, and a more dramatically different one, than future administrations can possibly present.

Even on Israel, where Republicans and Democrats start from similar positions, America's stance is a world away from much of Europe. America and Europe do not see the Middle East in the same way, and they are not going to do so. Their aims have never coincided, with the exception of Germany, whose sense of identity is entwined with Israel's success almost as much as is that of the United States. "The truth is that Europe is not anti-Israel," Tony Blair argued in an interview with *The Times* in May 2002. "Let's leave aside Britain for a moment, because we are known as friends of Israel. What is more prominent in Europe's political culture [than in America's] is a belief that the Palestinians have a raw deal. But that is not to say that Europe doesn't agree that Israel should exist."[4]

That is the best gloss which could be put on a difference of perspective that has been a constant source of friction. Democratic strategists say that Europe misunderstands them if it expects their party to perform the role that the center-left does in Europe; their affiliation to Israel is as deep as that of the Republicans. If Europe is expecting a sharp change from a Democratic president in that respect, it will be disappointed.

Europe will no doubt get something of what it wants in a president who sounds keener on working with other countries, but that could bring Europe itself new discomfort. It would produce demands — for military spending, for trade concessions — which Europe might not want to meet.

It is an insidious trap for Europe to set: to pretend that Bush was in every respect uniquely offensive, to set hopes for his successor so high, to ignore the real differences of interest, and then to condemn America once again for failing to fall in line with unrealistic expectations that deny that U.S. interests are different from those of Europe.

CONCLUSION:
THE CASE FOR OPTIMISM

The defense of America I have laid out is an argument for optimism. Relentless news reports of bombs, wars, and fear of recession make it easy to overlook how much has changed for the better in the past two decades, and how much that is underpinned by American actions. The oddity of the attacks on America is that they portray us as living in the worst of times, and yet they are made at a time when much is going well — and America deserves considerable credit for that.

Beyond dispute, Iraq is an ugly, shattered state which showed the limits of the world's most powerful military rather than advertising its strengths. True, America's project of exporting democracy has stalled amid derision. Yes, the turmoil of the financial markets seems to challenge America's great economic achievement.

But those disappointments do not profoundly challenge the principles and goals that have guided the American enterprise at home or abroad. The phrase "the proud American" is a source of limitless irritation outside the United States, but Americans have every reason to be proud. They have devised an enviable and humane way of organizing relations between themselves and built the world's most successful economic machine. You do not have to say that America has perfected itself — that it has arrived at "the end of history" — to acknowledge that achievement. It is impossible to overstate the influence of that record outside America's borders, in many of the dramatic changes for the better in the world of the last two decades alone.

The rise of China and India, the hundreds of millions of people who have been taken out of poverty in that time, the peaceful folding-in to Europe of former Soviet bloc countries, the opening up of the Soviet and Chinese markets which were formerly closed, the signs of progress and democracy in about half of Africa after decades of paralysis — these are astonishing developments, within less than a generation. In just five years, from 1999 to 2004, 135 million people stopped living in extreme poverty (living on one dollar a day or less). Almost half the world's population lives in a country growing at 7 percent a year or more; those economies will double in size in a decade. In the past twenty years, such changes have put in reach of billions of people a life of which their parents could not have dreamed. The United States can be credited with having brought about some of that change, by the attractions of its own success and openness, as well as by the direct benefits to others of its economic growth. Resentment of America has risen, but more have been converted to American principles of organization.

For some, this record of increasing prosperity means little when set against the troubles that dominate the headlines — in the Middle East, Afghanistan, Pakistan, and Russia — troubles, which, they argue, America has helped inflame. Of course, those threats are very serious. But at the moment, it is striking how contained they have remained, often with the help of America's presence. "Taliban with nukes," many call Pakistan, with unjustified exaggeration, ignoring how much of the country still works well. "The cauldron of conflict in the region," some have called Iraq after the American-led invasion, predicting a spreading conflagration that has not yet happened, however much the outcome has strengthened Iran's hand. So far, the troubles in these countries affect their own people more than any others, although there is justified worry that they could spread. Terrorism might make people in affluent countries feel directly under threat in a way that they were not before, but the real risk to their lives, or even lifestyles, is small.

That is not to make light of the horrors for those living in turmoil, nor to dismiss these upheavals as "small wars." But many can be contained, even if a political settlement and real peace take far longer, and even if the potential for conflict to spread wider remains a risk. Kosovo, East Timor, and Sierra Leone are the examples just from recent years. Those who look back with nostalgia to the supposed simplicity of the Cold War, arguing that it kept a lid on such conflicts, ignore how many battles were sparked as the superpowers jostled for advantage.

Many would seize on environmental worries—and American pollution—as the next threat to this picture of optimism. Perhaps; and the case for action on climate change is beyond dispute. Population growth and the admirable desire for development in poor countries will push up carbon emissions. Yet the history of societies' reaction to large threats, environmental, medical, or political, is indeed to react late but then to move with ingenuity and speed. That is certainly America's own tendency. You have to take an extraordinarily bleak view of the innovation of the past two centuries, and of the leaps in sophistication, to think that people will find no solutions. It is too magical, too punitive, and too moralistic to pronounce that the self-indulgence of humanity (or even just of America) has unleashed natural forces that cannot now be controlled and whose effects cannot be mitigated.

Many who take that pessimistic view about the environment seem to be hoping for confirmation of their underlying belief that there are inevitable limits to growth, whether imposed by radical climate change, exhaustion of natural resources, lack of water, or soaring population. Conflict will inevitably follow, they maintain; it is now a regular assertion in British government policy that climate change will cause the wars of the future. The potential for this is there, clearly, but again, this prophecy seems driven by a bleak view of people's ability to avoid conflict. Prosperity and development are easily blamed for causing clashes, but they also create the conditions of hope and optimism which make countries able to compromise, within their own societies and with one another.

That is the United States' own experience. For all the caricature of its critics that it is a society riven with racial hatred and historic guilt over slavery, unwilling to pay for the medical treatment of its poorest, unable to face the rising cost of its elderly, it has taken huge steps toward reconciling these old conflicts.

It might seem incongruous to point to world stock markets as a barometer of well-being. But they do express investors' carefully considered view of future growth and welfare. The calculation tries to take account of all the threats and uncertainties I have mentioned, from the price of oil, to global warming, to the risk of war or terrorist attack. In spring 2008, the Dow Jones Industrial Average was still significantly above the level before September 11, 2001, despite the slump which immediately followed that attack, the end of the technology boom, and the slowdown of the American economy in 2008. That represents investors' belief that the prospects for prosperity and stability are no worse now than they were before the attack that so changed America's view of itself and its enemies.

Iraq is largely to blame for the blow to American confidence in the twenty-first century. That is deserved; however great the national trauma of 9/11, it was a profound misjudgment to direct the retaliation at an unconnected country, and a cascade of other misjudgments then followed. But the second tragedy of that invasion, after the grief and fear it has caused to Iraqis, would be if the United States were to lose confidence in the value of promoting its own ideals and principles of government.

It might now temper that with more realism, more tact, and an acknowledgment that it has not perfected its own government. But after a century of success which was rightly called the American Century, the United States has every reason still to advocate the American way.

ACKNOWLEDGMENTS

Thanks above all to Geoff Shandler, my editor at Little, Brown, and to Ed Victor, my agent, for their enthusiasm for the idea. I owe Geoff particular thanks for his shrewdness in bringing the deadline forward, and to his colleagues Junie Dahn, Karen Landry, and Betsy Uhrig for their patience, precision, and speed in making the production possible in such a short time. At that point I should perhaps thank Bill Gates for creating the software — and the international near-monopoly — to make the layers of transatlantic editing so effortless.

Deep thanks also to my editors at *The Times,* James Harding, Robert Thomson, and Peter Stothard, who have provided hours of congenial and stimulating debate on just these topics — and who are staunchly in sympathy with those who try to defend America. Thanks, too, to Ben Preston, who as an endlessly energetic deputy editor of *The Times* commissioned many of the pieces which led to this book, and to my colleagues Michael Evans, defense editor, Zahid Hussain, Pakistan correspondent, and Stephen Farrell (now in Baghdad for the *New York Times*), who were generous in passing on their specialist knowledge with such enthusiasm. Also to Daniel Finkelstein, op-ed editor, for such reliable willingness to argue any point with passion, and Gill Ross, for sharing an office with me with such good humor and having to hear too many yelps of frustration about the process of finishing the text.

Most of all, perhaps, I should thank my colleagues Tom Rhodes and Ian Brodie, who shared the Washington bureau of *The Times* from 1996 to 1999 and who were such enjoyable company in the endgame of the Clinton administration. Tom, with laconic understatement, greeted me as I walked into the office on the morning that the Monica Lewinsky scandal broke by holding out the front page of the *Washington Post* and saying, "There's this," knowing that it had smashed all our plans for the week (and for the year, as it turned out). Ian, who sadly died in May 2008 and is much missed, kept us permanently alert by his propensity for proposing "to dash off a little piece, something to stop my fingers rusting up"; we would open the paper the next morning to find that a wickedly written anecdote about Strom Thurmond or another overcolorful Senate figure dominated the pages, while our stories were consigned to the margin.

I'm enormously grateful, too, to those friends who gave encouragement and read early sections: Professor Diane Roberts, now at Florida State University; Carla Power, Daniel Wolf, Shami Chakrabarti, and my brother Bruno, living in New York. Also to Ann Satterthwaite, a warm friend and neighbor in Washington, DC, who helped me fight off jet lag sitting up through the Obama-Clinton primary results, and to Maureen Howard and Mark Probst, who kindly had me and my daughter to stay in New York while I was finishing the proposal for this book.

On a professional note, there are many in the British Foreign Office, Downing Street, and the State Department, and the serving military of both countries, who would not want to be thanked by name; if they will forgive me a collective thanks, it is warmly given. Moving on to those who are inured to being professionally thanked and will not take it as implying anything about their own views, I am particularly grateful to a sequence of British ambassadors in Washington for conversations about transatlantic relations: Lord Kerr, Sir Christopher Meyer, Sir David Manning, and Sir Nigel Sheinwald, and to Sir John Sawers, British ambassador to the United Nations. Also to Robert Tuttle, U.S. ambassador in London, and to Gérard Errera,

France's ambassador; Wolfgang Ischinger, Germany's, and to Dr. Maleeha Lodhi, Pakistan's high commissioner, for many thoughtful comments in the years after September 11, 2001. I must add to that Devon Cross, for bringing such an impressive and timely list of those involved in policymaking in Iraq and beyond to her Policy Forum in London; similarly, Sir Jeremy Greenstock, former British ambassador to the United Nations and now director of the Ditchley Foundation (of which I am a governor), for invaluable conferences on the same theme; also Dr. Robin Niblett, director of Chatham House, and Dr. John Chipman, director-general of the International Institute for Strategic Studies, for attracting a constant stream of speakers of the kind who make London an unmatchable place from which to write about foreign affairs.

For comments with the general thrust of "it's not that simple," I should like to thank Mariot Leslie, Lieutenant-General Jonathon Riley, Daniel Bethlehem, and Antony Blinken; for undiluted exposition of their views, Tom Burke, on the environment, Colonel Dwight Sullivan, on the Guantánamo military commissions, and John Bolton, on Iran. I am enormously grateful, too, to the help from fellow journalists and from academics, particularly Carol Rosenberg of the *Miami Herald,* Dan Balz of the *Washington Post,* Michael

Goldfarb, Stephanie Koury, Dan Plesch, and Charles Ferguson.

I am grateful above all to my parents not just for provoking this—I can't say inspiring it, because they may well disagree with the text — but also for looking after my daughter when deadlines loomed (and I wouldn't want to miss a chance to thank the BBC's exceptionally intelligent CBeebies Channel for young children). On that note, I have to thank Laura for putting up with the enterprise with more patience than a five-year-old need do, and also for her interested and quizzical first reactions to the United States. After inspecting Manhattan's American Museum of Natural History, she wondered why so many dinosaurs had lived in New York; during the 2008 primaries, she suddenly declared (with no parental guidance, I must say), "I want the girl to win." I couldn't face telling her that, of all the ways in which America confounds its admirers and critics abroad, its regularly startling choice of presidents tops the list.

NOTES

Chapter 1: Why America Needs a Defense

1. Antony Blinken, discussion with Bronwen Maddox, November 2006.
2. Said during an interview with Bronwen Maddox for *The Times*, May 5, 1998.
3. Matthew Parris, "Yes, America's My Friend. Or Is It? Suddenly I'm Not Sure," *The Times*, January 13, 2007.
4. David Miliband, discussions and speeches on democracy, early 2008.

Chapter 2: Unloved, or Simply Loathed

1. For example, among Lewis's many books on the theme, *What Went Wrong?: The Clash Between Islam and Modernity in the Middle East* (New York: HarperCollins, 2003).
2. Marina Warner, *New York Times Magazine*, June 8, 1997.
3. Josef Joffe, "America the Inescapable," *New York Times Magazine*, June 8, 1997.
4. Nicolas Sarkozy, speech at the invitation of the French-American Foundation, Washington, DC, April 18, 2007, http://www .ambafrance-us.org/news/ (under "France/U.S. Relations").
5. Pew Global Attitudes Project, Pew Research Center, June 2007, http://pewglobal.org/reports/display.php?ReportID=256.
6. Ibid.
7. Ibid.

8. Transatlantic Trends 2007, http://www.transatlantictrends.org.

9. Margaret Drabble, "I Loathe America, and What It Has Done to the Rest of the World," *Daily Telegraph,* May 8, 2003.

10. Justin Webb, quoted in "From Seesaw to Wagon Wheel: Safeguarding Impartiality in the Twenty-first Century," report by the BBC Trust, June 2007.

11. BBC online debate on anti-Americanism, April 16, 2006, http://news.bbc.co.uk/1/hi/uk/4881474.stm.

12. Michael Werz and Barbara Fried, "Modernity, Resentment, and Anti-Americanism," in *Anti-Americanism: History, Causes, Themes,* vol. 1 (Westport, CT: Greenwood World Publishing, 2007).

13. Tony Blair, interview with Robert Thomson and Bronwen Maddox, *The Times,* May 21, 2002.

14. Peter Beinart, *New Republic,* July 2, 2001.

15. Peter Schneider, *New York Times Magazine,* June 8, 1997.

16. Alexander Stephan, ed., *The Americanization of Europe: Culture, Diplomacy, and Anti-Americanism After 1945* (New York: Berghahn Books, 2006).

17. George Orwell, "Raffles and Miss Blandish," 1944.

18. Hugh Wilford, "Britain: In Between," in *The Americanization of Europe,* 25.

19. Walter Mead, *Foreign Affairs,* March/April 2003.

20. Quoted in Jean-François Revel, *Anti-Americanism* (San Francisco: Encounter Books, 2003), 52.

21. David Martinon, quoted in the *New York Times,* October 28, 2007.

22. *Le Figaro,* August 28, 2007.

23. Bernard Kouchner, interview with Roger Cohen, *International Herald Tribune,* March 12, 2008.

24. *New York Times,* October 28, 2007.

25. Richard Haass, *Financial Times,* December 19, 2007.

26. Comments by Prime Minister Donald Tusk and Foreign Minister Radoslaw Sikorski in January 2008, including Sikorski, January 5, to the Polish paper *Gazeta Wyborcza:* "This is an American, not a Polish project."

Chapter 3: American Values Are Western Values

1. U.S. Census Bureau, 1992, http://www.census.gov/Press-Release/cb95-18.txt.

2. Jonathan Freedland, *Bring Home the Revolution* (London: Fourth Estate, 1999), 19.

3. David McCullough, *John Adams* (New York: Simon & Schuster, 2001).

4. Robert Kagan, *Of Paradise and Power: America and Europe in the New World Order* (New York: Knopf, 2003).

5. U.S. Census Bureau, 2000 Census, CIA World Factbook.

6. Michael Werz and Barbara Fried, "Modernity, Resentment, and Anti-Americanism," in *Anti-Americanism: History, Causes, Themes,* vol. 1 (Westport, CT: Greenwood World Publishing, 2007).

7. Jack Straw, said to Bronwen Maddox on Straw's chartered flight.

8. Office of Immigration Statistics, *2006 Yearbook of Immigration Statistics,* "Persons Obtaining Legal Permanent Resident Status by Region and Selected Country of Last Residence, Fiscal Years 1820 to 2006."

9. Giles Whittell, *The Times,* July 7, 2007.

10. Pew Research Center, "U.S. Religious Landscape Survey," February 25, 2008, http://pewresearch.org/pubs/743/united-states-religion.

11. George Weigel, February 22, 2006.

12. The legislative program of parliament is set by the government, and if the government's party has a majority in the Commons, its bills will pass. The House of Lords, the other chamber of parliament, has not been able to veto legislation since the Parliament Acts of 1911 and 1949; it can only revise and stall it. No monarch asked to give royal assent has threatened to withhold it since Queen Anne in 1708.

13. Said in conversation with Bronwen Maddox.

14. Fareed Zakaria, *Newsweek,* January 14, 2008.

15. Lord Kerr of Kinlochard, interview with Bronwen Maddox, *The Times,* May 27, 2005.

16. Said in conversation with Bronwen Maddox.

17. Ramachandra Guha, *India After Gandhi: The History of the World's Largest Democracy* (New York: HarperCollins, 2007).

Chapter 4: For Richer, For Poorer

1. George Soros, "The Worst Market Crisis in Sixty Years," *Financial Times,* January 23, 2008.
2. The Coca-Cola Company, Annual Report 2006, Form 10K.
3. *Fortune,* July 23, 2007.
4. Gunnar Öquist, October 4, 2006, when America won all the science Nobel Prizes that week.
5. Stefan Theil, *Foreign Policy,* January/February 2008.
6. *The Economist,* January 31, 2008.
7. Said at a conference of the Social Democratic Party, of which Müntefering was chairman, April 13, 2005.
8. Martin Wolf, *Why Globalization Works* (New Haven, CT: Yale University Press, 2004).
9. Paul Collier, *The Bottom Billion* (New York: Oxford University Press, 2007).
10. Peter Mandelson, Alcuin Lecture, Cambridge University, February 8, 2008.
11. The Coca-Cola Company, Annual Report 2006.
12. Michael Werz and Barbara Fried, "Modernity, Resentment, and Anti-Americanism," in *Anti-Americanism: History, Causes, Themes,* vol. 1 (Westport, CT: Greenwood World Publishing, 2007).
13. Quoted in *Newsweek,* September 10, 2007.
14. Ibid.
15. Jeremy Tunstall, *The Media Were American: U.S. Mass Media in Decline* (New York: Oxford University Press, 2007).
16. Quoted in *Financial Times,* February 20, 2008.

Chapter 5: The Pursuit of Democracy

1. John Quincy Adams, speech to the U.S. House of Representatives, July 4, 1821.
2. Albert J. Beveridge, speech, "In Support of an American Empire," 56th Cong., 1st sess., *Congressional Record,* 704–12.

3. George McKenna, *The Puritan Origins of American Patriotism* (New Haven, CT: Yale University Press, 2007).

4. Rudyard Kipling, "The White Man's Burden: The United States and the Philippine Islands," *McClure's Magazine,* February 1899.

5. Thomas Donnelly, *Empire of Liberty: The Historical Underpinnings of the Bush Doctrine* (Washington, DC: AEI, June 2005).

6. George W. Bush, Overview of America's National Security Strategy, http://www.whitehouse.gov/nsc/nss/2006/sectionI.html.

7. Niall Ferguson, *Financial Times,* January 26–27, 2008.

8. If there is space for one more, then the prize, in my view, should go to Francisco Goldman's *The Art of Political Murder,* an investigation into the 1998 assassination of a Guatemalan bishop who had helped lay the blame mainly on the country's military governments for the murders of an estimated 200,000 civilians. Francisco Goldman, *The Art of Political Murder* (London: Atlantic Books, 2008).

Chapter 6: Arrogant But Not Lawless

1. Said in conversation with Bronwen Maddox, March 2008.

2. Robin Givhan, the *Washington Post*'s inimitable style writer, April 15, 2005.

3. John Bolton, in a speech to a 1994 Global Structures Convocation hosted by the World Federalist Association (now Citizens for Global Solutions).

4. The forty-nine countries named by the White House as the "coalition of the willing" were Afghanistan, Albania, Angola, Australia, Azerbaijan, Bulgaria, Colombia, Costa Rica, Czech Republic, Denmark, Dominican Republic, El Salvador, Eritrea, Estonia, Ethiopia, Georgia, Honduras, Hungary, Iceland, Italy, Japan, Kuwait, Latvia, Lithuania, Republic of Macedonia, Marshall Islands, Micronesia, Mongolia, Netherlands, Nicaragua, Palau, Panama, Philippines, Poland, Portugal, Romania, Rwanda, Singapore, Slovakia, South Korea, Spain, Tonga, Turkey, Uganda, Ukraine, United Kingdom, United States, and Uzbekistan. Of these, the following countries had an active

or participant role, by providing either significant troops or political support: Australia, Bulgaria, Czech Republic, Denmark, Hungary, Italy, Japan, Latvia, Lithuania, Netherlands, Philippines, Poland, Portugal, Romania, Slovakia, Spain, Turkey, Ukraine, United Kingdom, and United States.

5. Interviews with U.S. officials, Bronwen Maddox, February 2007.

6. Glenn Prickett, quoted by Thomas Friedman, *International Herald Tribune,* September 27, 2007.

Chapter 7: The Iraq Invasion: Stupid But Not Malign

1. The case that Iraq failed most of the tests of a just war is made powerfully in *Just War* by Sir Michael Quinlan, the former permanent under-secretary (or most senior nonpolitical civil servant) of Britain's Ministry of Defence, and General Lord Guthrie of Craigiebank, the former chief of the defense staff and commander of NATO's Northern Army Group. *Just War* (London: Bloomsbury, 2007).

2. That case—for an early handover of sovereignty—is made by Jonathan Steele, the distinguished *Guardian* correspondent, in *Defeat: Why America and Britain Lost Iraq* (Berkeley, CA: Counterpoint, 2008).

3. In his book *Bad Days in Basra* (London: I. B. Tauris, 2008).

4. Barbara Bodine, quoted in *No End in Sight,* documentary, directed by Charles Ferguson of the Council on Foreign Relations, Red Envelope Entertainment, 2007.

Chapter 8: The Indefensible: Guantánamo and Torture

1. February 13, 2008, http://www.timesonline.co.uk.

2. As of March 2008, according to the Department of Defense: Ibrahim Ahmed, Mahmoud Al Qosi, Ghassan Abdullah Al Sharbi, Mohammed Ahmed Binyam, Omar Ahmed Khadr, David Matthew Hicks, Abdul Zahir, Sufyian Barhoumi, Salim Ahmed Salim Hamdan, Jabran Said Wazar Al Qahtani, Khalid Sheikh Mohammed, Walid Bin Attash, Ramzi Binalshibh, Ali Abd al-

Aziz Ali, Mustafa Ahmad al-Hawsawi, Mohammed al-Qahtani, Ahmad Al Darbi, Ali Hamza Al Bahlul, and Mohammed Jawad.

3. Donald Rumsfeld, said to reporters when touring Guantánamo base, January 28, 2002; George W. Bush, separate from Rumsfeld, January 28, 2002.

4. Colonel Morris Davis, quoted in the *Bradenton Herald,* February 28, 2006. "Remember if you dragged Dracula out into the sunlight he melted? Well, that's kind of the way it is trying to drag a detainee into the courtroom."

5. Colonel Morris Davis, in interviews in February 2008, including remarks published in the *New York Times,* February 28, 2008.

6. Decided June 29, 2006, http://www.supremecourtus.gov/opinions.

7. Confirmed dead, reported dead, or reported missing, compiled by the Associated Press, http://www.september11victims.com.

8. CIA head Michael Hayden, February 5, 2008, accompanying National Intelligence Director Mike McConnell in his annual threat assessment to the Senate Intelligence Committee. "We used it against these three detainees [Khalid Sheikh Mohammed, Abu Zubaydah, and Abd al-Rahim al-Nashiri] because of the circumstances at the time. There was the belief that additional catastrophic attacks against the homeland were inevitable. And we had limited knowledge about Al Qaeda and its workings. Those two realities have changed."

9. *Washington Post,* February 12, 2008.

10. President Bush's message to the House of Representatives, in vetoing the Intelligence Authorization Act for Fiscal Year 2008.

11. Richard Armitage to Charlie Rose, *The Charlie Rose Show,* November 7, 2007, a sentiment he has also expressed widely in writing.

12. Lord Goldsmith, attorney general, speaking at a conference on international terrorism at the Royal United Services Institute in London, May 10, 2006.

13. *The Times* online (http://www.timesonline.co.uk), in response to Bronwen Maddox article on Guantánamo of February 13, 2008.

14. *The Economist,* September 22, 2007.

Chapter 9: Be Careful What You Wish For

1. Measured by purchasing power parity, a way of translating one currency into another while allowing for goods being much cheaper in one country — in this case, China — than in the other.
2. January 10, 2008, Beijing.
3. Ibid.
4. Shaukat Aziz, interview with Bronwen Maddox for *The Times*.
5. United Nations Development Program, 1999.
6. President Putin, interview with Bronwen Maddox for *The Times*, June 2007.
7. President Putin announced Russia's intention to suspend participation in the Conventional Armed Forces in Europe treaty on July 14, 2007.
8. Dinner address, January 14, 2007, Beijing, Global Development Network (an international group of think tanks).
9. Pan Yue, a deputy minister at the government's environmental watchdog, quoted by *The Economist*, March 15, 2008.
10. John Ikenberry, "The Rise of China and the Future of the West: Can the Liberal System Survive?" *Foreign Affairs,* January/February 2008.
11. CIA World Factbook.
12. Ibid.
13. *Newsweek,* October 6, 2007.
14. President Ahmadinejad's blog: http://www.ahmadinejad.ir.
15. Israeli army officer, in conversation with Bronwen Maddox, 2007.
16. Seyed Mohammad Hossein Adeli, to Bronwen Maddox, November 2005.
17. Michael Lind, "America Still Works," *Prospect,* February 2008.

Chapter 10: How America Could Help Itself

1. In response to a piece by Bronwen Maddox on the "arms race in space" on October 19, 2006.
2. *The Economist,* June 20, 2007.

3. Gary Samore and others, "Repairing the Damage: Possibilities and Limits of Transatlantic Consensus," Adelphi Paper 389, International Institute for Strategic Studies, Routledge, UK, U.S., and Canada, August 2007.
4. Tony Blair, interview with Robert Thomson and Bronwen Maddox, *The Times,* May 21, 2002.